INDEPENDENT DIPLOMAT

Crises in World Politics

TARAK BARKAWI
BRENDAN SIMMS
editors

GÉRARD PRUNIER
Darfur—the Ambiguous Genocide

MARK ETHERINGTON
Revolt on the Tigris

FAISAL DEVJI
Landscapes of the Jihad

AHMED HASHIM
Insurgency and Counter-Insurgency in Iraq

ERIC HERRING & GLEN RANGWALA
Iraq in Fragments

IAIN KING & WHIT MASON
Peace at Any Price—How the World Failed Kosovo

CARNE ROSS

Independent Diplomat

Dispatches from an Unaccountable Elite

Cornell University Press
Ithaca, New York

Originally published in the United Kingdom by
C. Hurst & Co. (Publishers) Ltd, London.

First published 2007 by Cornell University Press

ISBN 978 0 8014 4557 6

Printed in the United States of America

Librarians: Library of Congress Cataloging-in-Publication Data are available.

Cornell University Press strives to use environmentally responsible suppliers
and materials to the fullest extent possible in the publishing of its books. Such
materials include vegetable-based, low-VOC inks and acid-free papers that
are recycled, totally chlorine-free, or partly composed of nonwood fibers. For
further information, visit our website at www.cornellpress.cornell.edu.

Cloth printing   10 9 8 7 6 5 4 3 2 1

CONTENTS

Acknowledgements   *page* vii

1. Introduction   1
2. The Embassy   27
3. The Negotiation (1)   49
4. War Stories   71
5. Them and Us   83
6. The Telegram or How to Be Ignored   107
7. The Ambassador   129
8. Star Trek, Wittgenstein and the Problem with Foreign Policy   151
9. The Negotiation (2)   165
10. Independent Diplomat or the Other Side of the Table   187
11. Conclusion — The End of "Diplomacy"?   203

Notes   227
Index   239

To Karmen

ACKNOWLEDGEMENTS

There are a great many people I would like to thank for helping me prepare this book. Some helped in practical ways with research, reviews and advice. Others helped by talking with me, influencing my thinking or by simply listening. I am indebted to all of them. Any mistakes are, of course, my own responsibility.

I would like to thank in particular Michael Dwyer at Hurst for his encouragement and thoughtful criticism, which were invaluable, Roger Haydon at Cornell University Press, Maria Petalidou at Hurst, the editors of the Crises in World Politics series, Brendan Simms and Tarak Barkawi, and Rosemary Brook and Maja Zupan at Kaizo.

I am very grateful to Mike Cohen and Jonathan Bach at the New School University in New York, who first gave me space and time to think by inviting me to become a fellow at their Graduate Program on International Affairs. Others who have helped along the way, by reading drafts, undertaking research, discussing specific ideas or episodes, or in other ways, include Jonathan Agar, Ardian Arifaj, Asmaa Donahue, Vanessa Howe-Jones, Chris Kyriacou, Angela Lewis, Andrew Lloyd, William Maley, Edward Mason, Rebecca Mead, Tania Mechlenborg, Mark Roberts, Imran Shafi, Sarah Ross, Neal Sandin, Stephanie Thomas and Anthony Wilson. Inigo Thomas has been an unfailing friend in his encouragement and advice. I want to give special thanks to my friends Laila Parsons and Rob Wisnovsky, both now academics in Canada, who introduced me to the ideas of the discourse, the narrative and indeed

— essentially — essentialism. I have not enjoyed discussing the world, or ideas, with anyone more.

I wish to thank too the many people who have helped make the organisation Independent Diplomat a reality, including Patrick Shine and John Rafferty at Unltd; Di Stubbs, Stephen Pittam and the trustees of the Joseph Rowntree Charitable Trust; Aryeh Neier and George Soros of the Open Society Institute; Adrian Arena at the Oak Foundation; and ?Whatif! Innovation (particularly James Baderman, Paul Wilson and Kris Murrin in London, and Meldrum Duncan, Nina Powell and the crew who made me so welcome in NYC), all of whom have done so much to support and inspire Independent Diplomat. Unsung (until now) is the *pro bono* help we have very gratefully received from the international law firms Lovells and Cleary Gottlieb Steen & Hamilton LLP, New York University School of Law (in particular Simon Chesterman) and the International Senior Lawyers' Project (in particular Jean Berman and Eldon Greenberg). Paul Keetch MP, Jeremy Oppenheim at McKinsey, Olivier Kayser and Ben Metz at Ashoka and Baroness Frances d'Souza have given me very welcome moral support and practical advice. My father helped Independent Diplomat in the early tough days — I thank him. My cousin Stefanie Grant has been an unceasing and much-valued source of support and wisdom. Gratitude does not suffice for the board and staff of Independent Diplomat. They are the organisation; without them it could not exist.

I would also like to thank my former colleagues at the Foreign & Commonwealth Office, who taught me much about diplomacy, and some of whom taught me about much more. In particular I would like to thank Sir Jeremy Greenstock, Robert Cooper (now at the European Union), Alyson Bailes (now at SIPRI) and David Richmond, all of whom were, in different ways, kind, inspirational as well as instructive bosses. My criticisms of that institution, and the discourse of diplomacy (if I can call it that), are not of them, but of the system. I thank too my many friends in the FCO: I still miss their companionship.

Finally, I dedicate this book to my wife, Karmen, who has supported me and guided me in more ways than I can ever say. Without her, the journey this book represents simply would not have happened.

London, January 2007   C.R.

"War will be dead, the scaffold will be dead, frontiers will be dead, royalty will be dead, dogmas will be dead, man will begin to live."

Victor Hugo

1

INTRODUCTION

Back at the UN Security Council in New York. A cockpit of world affairs, this is also my workplace. The Council chamber and its maze of adjoining rooms and corridors are familiar to me. I know all its nooks and corners — where to make discreet phone calls reporting discussions back to London (or to my girlfriend), where to twist the arms of colleagues in private (this place was made for corridor diplomacy), the spot to grab a moment's peace without being bothered by other delegations or journalists (a former French ambassador once wrote a book on the best places to sleep at the UN: there were many). It feels like home ground.

The formal Council Chamber is located deep in the UN complex. To reach it you must make your own way through long corridors. There are no signposts; but I know the route well.

As I enter, I greet the Secretariat staff with whom I have worked for so long, "How are you? Fine." I recognise a couple of other diplomats; we chat briefly. I smile and wander into the chamber, smell its closed air (there are no windows). Dimly lit and soberly decorated, the Chamber exudes gravitas and high politics. The Council table dominates the room — a large, wooden U-shape surrounded by soft blue seats fixed to the floor in discrete groups (for the fifteen

Council members) around it. On the wall behind the table, a huge mural looms. Donated by Norway, it depicts machines and people in an unintelligible panorama, whose meaning, during long meetings, I have often fruitlessly questioned.

Inside the U is a long table, lowered below the rest of the room, where the Secretariat officials sit, barely observed as they annotate and record the meetings. To the side, five yards from the table, is an inclined bank of seats for UN states which are not Council members. Above them, and still further away, is a "public" gallery, though the public is only allowed in when no one is meeting here. A mini-geography of power and influence.

Without thinking I move towards a group of seats at the Council table, where the UK delegation has its place. But I must stop myself. I am no longer a British diplomat. There is no place for me at the table. Today I am a member of the Kosovo delegation. There is not even a nameplate for us here, since Kosovo is not a country recognised by the UN.

I swallow and look for seats at the side of the Council table, where other member states must sit to observe the "formal" Council meetings. On this occasion, and only this one, the Kosovars have been specially permitted to sit here, though no seats have been reserved for them. Even the Prime Minister, Bajram Kosumi, whose first official visit to the Council this is, must hunt for a place among the scattered junior diplomats who take notes at the Council's sessions. His interpreter, a volunteer from a nearby university, manages to sit behind him and whisper Albanian into his ear. No interpretation is provided for him, though it is the future of his country that is being discussed.

The Prime Minister, though head of a democratically-elected government, participates only as a member of an UNMIK (the UN Interim Administration Mission in Kosovo) delegation, led by an unelected UN official. He is not allowed near the Council table, unlike Boris Tadic, the President of Serbia, a country which was driven from any substantive authority over Kosovo in 1999. Humiliatingly, Tadic welcomes the presence of the "leader of Kosovo's Albanians" in the UN delegation; Kosumi is not permitted to respond.

Next to the Prime Minister, I sit and fidget in the non-Council seats, far from my former perch. I recall my days as a British diplomat on the Council, when I enjoyed a certain swagger. The P5 (the five permanent Council members) run the Council, and during the Council's formal meetings (of which this is one), I would march around the formal chamber, gossiping with my friends and colleagues, collecting intelligence on the moves of other Council members, passing notes to my ambassador and chatting with the Secretariat staff. I would go into their side-offices to borrow their computers to write speaking notes for my ambassador or copy draft statements to circulate. I would lounge expansively in the soft chairs provided for the delegations of the Council, fiddling with my notebook or mobile phone, always busy. It was our domain.

As an honorary Kosovar, I immediately feel intimidated by our humble rank in the Council's hierarchy. Walking by the burly security guards who stand at the doors to the chamber, I worry that my temporary UN protocol badge will not pass muster and that I will be denied entrance. Although I have much to ask the diplomats of the important Council delegations, I suddenly feel too nervous to bother them as they sweep around, as I once did, looking busy.

Seated away from and to the side of the Council table, I do not dare approach the delegations seated around it, as one would not inter-rupt a bishop during a service in his cathedral.

I try to recapture my former élan and confidence, but it is hard to re-muster. Instead, along with my timidity, I find frustration with those who sit at the Council table. Although their faces are anony-mous and their expressions bored, the diplomats of the Council annoy me: in them, of course, I recognise my former self. Their in-difference was once mine. I feel irritation on behalf of the Kosovars at their treatment. While the delegations of Argentina and Tanzania drone on with their stock phrases applicable to any conflict ("there must be greater efforts for reconciliation between the parties"), the Prime Minister, who had travelled five thousand miles to attend this discussion of his country's affairs, is not even permitted to speak.

His visit, which I have organised, has been an education. The UN assigned its most junior officials to make the arrangements. Our requests consequently take an age to process, as they must be referred upwards in that towering hierarchy. We ask to use the UN press room to brief journalists on this historic occasion: the first time that a Prime Minister of Kosovo has attended Security Council discussions of his country. We are told this is impossible, only to discover by chance that the UN's Special Representative is at this moment using the room for his own briefing.

When we request meetings, senior officials melt away ("he has an urgent engagement") to be replaced by more junior substitutes. The US ambassador refuses to see us: his underling says he has "no interest". The Austrian mission brusquely refuses to organise a meeting with the European Union's collected ambassadors (Austria is the EU's rotating President): "This has no precedent". We have

no recourse but to curse and sigh when we put down the phone. We are provided with no delegation room in which to organise ourselves and instead spend all our time in the delegates' coffee lounge (where to their relief the Kosovars can at least smoke).

When the British ambassador wants a meeting with the UN Secretary-General, it is always granted without delay. When Kosovo's Prime Minister wants one, it is not confirmed until the night before (the request was made weeks earlier); the audience itself lasts a brisk ten minutes. The Secretary-General's staff make clear to us that we are not to linger. Nevertheless, the Prime Minister, his picture taken for the Kosovo history books, is deeply grateful.

There are more subtle distinctions too. When I was with the British mission, officials of the UN or other countries paid attention when we spoke. Doubtless this was often faked, but it was perhaps felt to be required, given Britain's place in the UN pecking order. With the Kosovars, no such deference is necessary. Junior officials become impatient with our demands and even on occasion allow themselves a perceptible sneer when they talk to us. For them, it is acceptable behaviour to interrupt the Kosovo Prime Minister when he is talking, but how would these same people have behaved if the British Prime Minister had been within view? I find it thoroughly depressing. I ask the Kosovars how they feel. They say it is normal and that they are used to it.

On the last night of the visit, the vicissitudes and irritations at last behind us, we celebrate. A ridiculous stretch limo is rented for a couple of hours, and we cruise Manhattan, drinking vodka and dancing in our seats. Later, at an Albanian-American "Italian" restaurant, we drink and eat copiously. Amid the hubbub of Albanian voices, it is as if we are in Pristina. I am the only non-Kosovar there. The

Prime Minister sings anthems from his days as a political prisoner in Milosevic's Yugoslavia.

This is one privilege I had not expected. For the Prime Minister and his delegation, the visit is a proud moment in their country's progress, an achievement regardless of the frustrations. It is another step on the road to the ultimate liberation of independence.

Before the French revolution, according to Simon Schama in *Citizens*, Louis XVI's palace at Versailles "had been built around the ceremonial control of spectacle through which the mystique of absolutism was preserved and managed. At its centre, both symbolically and architecturally, was the closeted monarch. Access to his person was minutely described by court etiquette, and proximity or distance, audience or dismissal, defined the pecking order of the nobility permitted to attend him. The palace exterior facing the town expressed this calculated measurement of space and time by confronting the approaching visitor with a succession of progressively narrowing enclosures. From the stables and the Grand Commun housing the kitchens, where space was at a premium, to the 'marble court' at the centre of which the King's bedroom was housed, the visiting ambassador would negotiate a small series of pierced barriers or grilles, each one admitting a further measure of access."[†]

The United Nations headquarters on Manhattan's East Side is sadly no Versailles but the tall, slab-like block has a certain emphatic presence: its singular design (by Le Corbusier and others) is the

---

[†] Reproduced from CITIZENS: A CHRONICLE OF THE FRENCH REVOLUTION (Published by Viking/Alfred A. Knopf Inc., © Simon Schama 1989) by kind permission of PFD (www.pfd.co.uk) on behalf of Professor Simon Schama.

reason why the tour buses pause on First Avenue and the sightseeing cruises dawdle on the East River. As at Versailles, one only enters as a tourist or an invited guest. The latter-day equivalent of Versailles' barriers and grilles is the glass wall, through which the visitor can glimpse the vast General Assembly hall or the empty Security Council chamber (the public is not admitted when the Security Council is in session, even during its so-called "open" or "public" meetings). Meeting a national diplomat at the UN or a UN official is, like an audience with the King, a more difficult matter, its ease or difficulty a signifier of one's status in the obscure hierarchies of international diplomacy. Admittance to the UN's missions (the offices of the member states represented at the UN) or the Secretariat is by pre-arranged appointment only. To see even the most junior official, you must first know who they are (no easy matter in itself) and give them a compelling reason why they should meet you. As an ordinary member of the public, it is unlikely that you will be received by even the lowliest official. To meet an ambassador or an Under-Secretary of the UN, you must yourself enjoy an equivalent rank in diplomacy or politics (a minister or a senior parliamentarian perhaps) or business (in diplomacy, as elsewhere, money has its own special heft). Like Versailles' inner sanctum, the Secretary-General's suite lies in the most remote and inaccessible part of the Secretariat building, its summit, or the "thirty-eighth floor" as it is known to UN insiders. A special reserved lift will help you ascend to this peak, where, if your appointment is confirmed and credentials have sufficient weight, you will be ushered into a small waiting room, there to await the gift of the limited time of the Secretary-General.

The revolutionaries of 1789 (like those of 1917) tried to change the nature of their politics and indeed their diplomacy. They suc-

ceeded in the first task but not the second. The practice of diplomacy was impervious to revolutionary passion; it remains a closed
world, accessible only to an appointed élite, and intelligible only
through their codes and terminologies.

This practice is now massive and complex, globally ubiquitous
and present in almost every issue that concerns us in the modern
world. It covers both the more traditional business of bilateral
diplomacy — of one country's relations with another — and multilateral diplomacy: the world of the United Nations, the European or African Union, the WTO, G8, ASEAN and so on. It is a
discourse whose practices have been acquired over decades and
centuries, and with these practices have accumulated assumptions
and ways of thought which dominate today the way that diplomats
think and talk about their work, and indeed the way that others
(journalists, academics) think and consider diplomats' work too.
This book's examination of those practices and assumptions covers both worlds, the multilateral and the bilateral, for in both
the manner of thinking is similar, if not the same. The analysis is
drawn from my personal experience.

I have eschewed the contemporary controversies over the future
of the United Nations, or US unilateralism. These have been well
covered elsewhere. My suspicion is that even this debate is problematic in that it makes over-simplistic assumptions of what is going
on in the world. In a way, all such theories are deficient, in that
they are theories. As the Polish writer Witold Gombrowicz put it,
all theories are nets through which we strain life (ergo something
— perhaps something important — falls through the holes). Contemporary diplomacy is premised on such theories — of how states
behave, of realism, or neo-realism, or neo-conservatism — and

narrow ones at that, and that is their fundamental problem. If this book offers the reader an alternative theory, it is that there should be no theories, at least not ones that offer universalist explanations of international relations (even if, paradoxically, universalist approaches are just what the world needs, but we shall come to this). My critique maintains neither an internationalist nor a unilateralist view of the world (or it does both). It is aimed not so much at the UN Secretary-General (or the US President) but at the assumptions that inform their thinking and, perhaps above all, the succouring and affirming officials who surround them. These officials, and the way that they think, should be laid open to greater scrutiny and interrogation.

The lattice of multinational bodies and institutions that spans the globe is in some ways diplomacy's greatest achievement. A multinational, intergovernmental body now exists to arbitrate and sometimes legislate almost every conceivable aspect of our public lives, even the very air we breathe. The lattice is a reassuring presence. Its omnipresent embrace helps us to believe that the world's problems are being taken care of. The semiotics of these institutions reinforce this impression. A neat globe sits at the centre of the UN's symbol, the world's disorder ordered into a clear geometric circle and all inscribed upon a safe, neutral azure, suggestive perhaps of the sky, a clean ocean, indeterminate but certainly not ugly, bloody or discordant. In other institutions (the European Union, the World Trade Organisation) circled stars, mingled flags or entwined hands symbolise a vague and warm aspiration for cooperation and togetherness, even where none may exist. I am colour-blind but even I am calmed by these soft whites, deep blues and uniform tones and patterns.

The lattice has achieved great works: treaties to ban landmines, end global warming or protect children in wartime. Even if these paper promises remain unfulfilled, the international lattice has indeed contributed to ending conflict and to mobilising help for the poor or the disaster-struck. War is now much less prevalent than in the recent past, as a recent UN study has shown; and many people are richer and live longer and healthier lives than their forebears (although the precise determinants of these successes are of course moot).

However, the lattice incubates one terrible flaw, a harbinger of its own demise. This flaw is a deficit, even identified as such in the European Union as the "democratic deficit". The institutions which make up the lattice are like vast windowless bastions studding the landscape. Although their purposes may be good, their inhabitants are nameless and invisible, their workings too often unintelligible and hidden. While some may be well-intentioned and others idle or malign, the countless officials who inhabit these bastions share one indivisible characteristic — they are not accountable for their actions; indeed you will not know — with one or two rare exceptions — who they are. This criticism applies not only to the multilateral institutions of international diplomacy but equally to the foreign ministries of the world's most democratic countries.

Karl Popper spent his life considering the flaws and merits of democracy versus other less participative forms of government such as fascism and communism. He proved beyond argument that democracy was the best, if still imperfect, form of government. But his work concerned only individual states: how a particular country in isolation should be governed.

Today, our problems are global as well as local. We do not have world government but nor do we have world democracy. Instead we have an agglomeration of states cooperating sometimes well and sometimes badly to address their shared problems. Whatever the denizens of these organs of cooperation (the UN, the EU) may pretend, this is no democracy. And the failings that Popper identified in non-democratic governments afflict this system just as surely as they did the communist governments of eastern Europe which he so trenchantly criticised.

In a sentence, these afflictions are a lack of accountability and responsiveness to the problems the system is supposed to address. The governed have very little, if any, access to the governors of this system; still less do they have means to sway or influence them. If international policies go wrong, the mechanisms to feed back information on those failings are imperfect. For Popper this was the crucial component of a democracy: since society is complex and there is no perfect knowledge, government would always make mistakes: no government would always institute the right policies to solve society's problems. The only way to correct such mistakes was for the governed, through elections and other elements of the open society (a free press, the legal system, civil organisations), to inform the governors that their policies were not working and to propose how they might be changed. Such feedback mechanisms only exist in scant form in the field of international policy.

Those affected in country A by the policies of country B have no means of informing the policymakers of country B what is going wrong (or right). This problem is compounded in multilateral organs, where policymaking countries must perforce pay much more attention to the views of those with whom they must negoti-

ate to make policy, than to those affected by their shared policies on the ground (as I learned negotiating collective policy on Iraq at the UN).

This book is not only a theoretical (and anti-theoretical) analysis of the problems of contemporary diplomacy. It is also a personal account of my slow descent from illusion to disillusionment, followed by a return to belief or perhaps a new illusion — time will tell.

I became a diplomat, after one failed attempt, in 1989, when I joined what was then known as the "fast stream" of the British Foreign Office or Diplomatic Corps. It was the fulfilment of a long-held ambition, fuelled in part by a fascination with the world and a desire to escape suburban banality, and in part by pure ambition: for status, esteem and recognition. Diplomacy offered an elegant combination of the two.

I duly loved my work and "the office", as the Foreign Office was known. Its rituals and habits — the thick green memo paper, the elaborate protocols for visiting statesmen or ministers — delighted me, and I was quick to immerse myself in them. What I failed to notice was my parallel immersion in the ways of thought that permeate such institutions. As my posture became more proudly upright, so too did I begin to talk of how "we" saw the world, "we" being Britain, which I now was encouraged to embody. My self, and its individual conscience, was slowly suborned into the collective, and the collective's way of thinking, which was of a world of states and interests: something very different from the personal morality and conscience which had hitherto formed my mental architecture.

I undertook the usual round of postings — Norway, Germany, the UK Mission in New York — and jobs: in London I was variously

desk officer working on Benelux,[1] the Iraq/Kuwait or "Gulf" war of
1990, the global environment, the Arab/Israel dispute; I was also
for a while, and unhappily, speechwriter for the Foreign Secretary.
My career prospered, but as it did so a shadow began to form across
my experience. I tried to ignore it, and became in response all the
more vigorous in the aggressive pursuit of my country's goals and
thus of my career. This conflict came to a head during what was to
be my last full posting for the British foreign service when I was First
Secretary at the UK Mission to the United Nations in New York
(1997-2002).

My work in New York was hard; the long hours helped me to
conceal, or rather allowed me to deny, some deeper contradictions
in my work. Imbued with the self-serving belief of many western
diplomats (and, I suspect, particularly British and American ones),
I truly believed that "our" policy in the Middle East, for which I was
responsible in New York, was good and right. This assumption was
helped by the fact that I had only rarely visited the region (and spoke
none of its languages), and had never visited (and never did visit) the
place for which I was primarily responsible, Iraq itself.

I was directly responsible for Britain's policy towards Iraq at the
UN — mainly in the Security Council, both weapons inspections
and sanctions ("responsible" here is a problematic word, because
although I was in a direct and personal way responsible, in the way
governments and civil servants think about policy, my ministers
were responsible and not I myself). This policy, like most policies,
was a complicated story, where good and bad were sometimes hard
to distinguish. And it is only after years of reflection that I have
reached some clarity about my experiences at this time — and even

this may be merely a sieving, a reduction, and thus a deception of its own kind.

My job was to prepare and negotiate resolutions — international law — on Iraq, the bits of paper that obliged all countries to stop exports and imports to and from Iraq (sanctions) and for Iraq to prove the disarmament of its Weapons of Mass Destruction.[2] Slowly, I became horribly aware that what "we" were doing in Iraq, namely enforcing sanctions, was achieving the wrong objective, namely harming ordinary people. Saddam's manipulations contributed to this, but our own policy reinforced this effect. Meanwhile, I became steeped in the complex lore and technologies of unconventional weapons and their delivery systems, all the better to argue that Saddam had not disarmed. I could name the different variants and capabilities of Scud missiles; I could describe the degradation process of VX nerve agent; I knew the units and numbers of Saddam's special weapons regiments. This knowledge helped me perform my job with vigour — I became proud (to my present shame) of my Rottweiler-like reputation at the Security Council, as the most effective and aggressive defender of British-American Iraq policy, sanctions and all. I could demolish anyone's contrary arguments with a devastating barrage of carefully-chosen facts. But this knowledge was also to prove my nemesis as a diplomat.

Exhausted and troubled by my work at the UN, I took a sabbatical from mid-2002 at the New School University in New York, to which I am forever grateful. From this close vantage point, and still in close touch with many former colleagues (including diplomats on the Security Council and other experts like David Kelly, with whom I had organised many briefings on Iraq's weapons), I watched the British and American governments, and my former colleagues in

both (diplomats from the two countries worked in very close concert on this issue), deploy arguments for war. Here my knowledge was my undoing, since I was immediately aware that the case for war presented by Washington and London was a gross exaggeration of what we knew (I had said so, in the mild terms employed in officialdom, when asked to comment on the early drafts of what later became known as the infamous Number Ten dossier). Moreover, Britain's behaviour in the Security Council was at best manipulative and at worst dishonest, as one resolution (1441) was sold to the Council as the "last chance for peace" to get the inspectors back in. Then, prematurely and before our own deadlines (which I had helped design and negotiate in the establishment of the weapons inspection agency UNMOVIC[3]), we declared that Iraq was "not cooperating" (another exaggeration, this time of what the inspectors had said). Failing to win the authority from the Security Council with a further resolution (the famously failed "second resolution"), my former colleagues declared that the first resolution (the "last chance for peace") had given them the necessary authority to go to war in any case.

In all my career, I had been taught and believed that Britain stood not only for a world of rules but also for that more ineffable quality of integrity. Many will think me disingenuous, but this was the rock on which I based myself as a diplomat, even when contradictions presented themselves, as they often had. But this was too much.

However, my attachment to my identity as a diplomat was so great that I could not tear myself away, despite my anguish at the behaviour of my government and colleagues. I drafted many resignation letters but did not send them. That summer David Kelly killed himself after telling journalists what I too had been telling them,

although his experience as a scientist gave him much more authority than me, a mere diplomat. His suicide appalled and enraged me. My anguish deepened but not my decisiveness. I vacillated between resignation and the self-interest of my career. To postpone the choice, I went to Kosovo on secondment to the UN mission there. In the summer of 2004, I testified to the official inquiry into the use of intelligence on Iraq's WMD, conducted by Lord Butler. Indicative of my ambivalence, my testimony was delivered in secret (I am listed as a witness with no name) so as not to undermine my career. But the act of testifying was a kind of epiphany. Setting down my views (that the case for war was exaggerated, that there was a viable alternative to war) at last hardened my resolve. Shortly after giving my testimony to Butler, I sent it to the Foreign Secretary as my resignation from the British diplomatic service (he did not reply).

Tempting though it is, it would be dishonest to claim that Iraq was the only reason for my departure. The narrative of the brave official resigning in protest at the dishonesty of his government is a familiar, and seductive, one. But in my case it was only part of the truth (and a part which I have played on). There were other forces at work.

In my sabbatical year, I had investigated the philosophy of knowledge: how it is that we come to claim that certain things are true. This was an exercise designed to help answer my doubts about the whole discourse of diplomacy. Both in its practice and its terms, diplomacy for me had stopped seeming "real". I was weary, disillusioned and often bored, even though the subjects I was dealing with — Iraq, Afghanistan, terrorism — were among the most important and exciting in the world. Diplomacy can seem intensely glamorous. Television crews would chase me down corridors to get the latest

on the P5 talks on Iraq; people I met at cocktail parties would nod approvingly when I told them my job. But there was considerable drudgery too. Negotiation in the UN Security Council, but also my day-to-day work as a diplomat in the ministry at home and embassies overseas, seemed both literally and figuratively disconnected from the issues it was supposed to be arbitrating. My life was feeling desiccated and more and more meaningless.

My investigation began into the utility of terms, and thus of language, and indeed of all symbols and theories, to explain reality. This quickly led me to an understanding of their limits and a realisation about diplomatic terms: that the words permitted in diplomacy are but a subset of a broader language, itself a subset — a reduction — of reality. A sub-set of a sub-set can feel narrow indeed. And I began to suspect that this narrowness was part of the problem with diplomacy itself, especially when diplomacy was attempting to deal with more and more of the world's problems: our reality.

My work in New York had revealed other problems too, both personal and political, with the profession of diplomacy. I enjoyed questioning and arguing with senior colleagues and ministers but for my career to reach the peak, I would have to set limits on such behaviour. I noticed that the senior members of Britain's foreign service never questioned the instructions of their ministers (and certainly never the Prime Minister), or if they did, it was in such timid and allusive terms that one could fail to notice that any concern was being raised at all. One ambassador discouraged me from raising questions (internally) about the direction of an item of policy in a telegram (the main form of communication in the Foreign Office) but instead suggested I put my questions in the form of a personal letter which would not of course be seen by ministers or, unlike

a telegram, be signed off by him — even though he fully agreed with all that I wanted to say.

The smart suits and ties I wore as a diplomat began to feel more restrictive and more uncomfortable. I realised that the separate identities I had maintained, as me and my professional diplomatic self, would have to merge, and with that union something very important would be lost.

There was also, not only in the British service, but among all of those with whom I interacted as a formal diplomat, a profound commitment to a particular way of talking and thus thinking about things: the discourse. In my first few years as a diplomat, I loved talking about the world in this way — of German interests, of Russia's next move, of how "we" might outwit the French (a perennial British favourite), of alliances and mutual interests — much as in earlier years, I had loved the boardgame "Diplomacy": a world of coloured pieces, them and us, with discrete interests and options, which could be engineered and moved around to create discord or harmony. When French diplomats told me what France wanted, I took them at their word, as I hoped they would take me at mine when I talked of what "we" — Britain — wanted. But as time went on, this seemed to me more and more ridiculous — a fabrication. And as I reflected on the process that allowed us as diplomats to say "Britain wants this" or "the US wants that", the more I realised that this was an arbitrary and manufactured process, with little grounding in reality, and certainly only very rarely discussed with those in whose name the whole discourse was being practised. In other words, something of a sham.

There was a deeper moral concern at play too. The performance of diplomacy is founded on a particular view of the world — one

of competition, of nation states, of limited resources, of agreement or contest. And like all political philosophies, this is premised on a singular view of mankind: the "Hobbesian" notion that people just want more, and are ultimately self-seeking and power-hungry (Hobbes is explicit on this point), and that the only source of stability and order and harmony is the state (although paradoxically the state is allowed to do things — like kill and imprison — which are forbidden for individuals).

In my work on Iraq, and later in Kosovo, I began to doubt this view and wondered why I should spend my life working for one group of people — British — when there were others who were suffering much more than we were. Our self-assigned identity as bringers of democracy, rights and other goods was sufficient only up to a certain point (and especially when, as with sanctions against Iraq, it was not clear that we were bringing good at all). This separation of us, my country, from the rest of humanity began to seem false and invidious, elevating "our" needs above "theirs". Moreover, working in these places I realised something very obvious — that there are a great many people who are ignored and marginalised in the closed world of diplomacy, and often — indeed usually — these are the ones suffering most. When I sat in negotiation with the Kosovars or Palestinians, I began to yearn to be on their side of the table rather than my own. Romantic perhaps, but to me that began to have a greater source of meaning than the predictable ascent up the career ladder (and partly that predictability was a disincentive too).

In my reading on my sabbatical, there was one passage, in one book, which stuck in my mind. In Ray Monk's outstanding biography of Ludwig Wittgenstein, he describes an incident in the early

days of the Second World War when Wittgenstein and a colleague noticed a news story that Britain had instigated a recent assassination attempt on Hitler. Wittgenstein's colleague commented that "the British were too civilised and decent to attempt anything so underhand, and such an act was incompatible with the British 'national character'". Wittgenstein was furious: even five years later, he complained to the colleague at the "primitiveness" of the remark. It occured to me that such beliefs continued to underpin the national self-image chosen and perpetuated by diplomats like me. It followed that it made little sense to choose to serve one group over another: "us" rather than "them".

There is something wrong in the state of diplomacy. This book elaborates eight related problems, which are connected and compound one another. Together they have created a discourse which is profoundly flawed and inapposite for the problems of the world.

1. Diplomacy is not democratic, even in democracies. Somehow, and through the accretions of practice and habits of history, it is accepted that diplomats are a separate élite, who are free to arbitrate policy with little outside scrutiny, influence or accountability. We the governed and those affected by their decisions have little idea what the diplomats are doing in our name, or even who they are. This is true of the US State Department; it is even more true of the Chinese foreign ministry. The juxtaposition is deliberate. Even in supposed democracies, it is very difficult to know what our representatives are doing in our name. It is all but impossible to have access to them or influence their decisions; if they make mistakes, which will inevitably happen, it is only very rarely possible to hold these practitioners to account.

2. The identification between the diplomats and their state is a false and arbitrary one. When you become a diplomat, you are encouraged to submit yourself to the collective state: your individual "I" becomes "we". Members of the diplomatic elite are encouraged and taught to see themselves as the embodiment of their state (not merely their government), as in "We [Britain] believe that Iran should immediately allow access to its nuclear sites." The justification for such identification — that the diplomats represent the government which represents the state whose population has elected the government — is tenuous. In reality, the identification is a disguise for arbitrary, manufactured and unaccountable decision-making. When a diplomat speaks as "we" that statement only very rarely has anything to do with the real collective wishes of the state concerned. The "we" is also problematic in that it encourages individual diplomats to subsume their own personal morality into that of the state. This therefore permits amoral behaviour since by conventional thinking the state has no morality and is free to do things that the individual is not free to do.

3. This problem is closely allied to another. Despite the falsity of the élite's adoption of the interests of the state as their own, and the appropriation to themselves of the right to decide what is best for that state, the population concerned often seems to accept this role. Their passivity is the necessary corollary. Perhaps this too is an historical inheritance — that many people seem to accept that they should be excluded from the arbitration of their own affairs internationally. But perhaps it also serves their own interest. There is an unspoken, unacknowledged pact at work: the diplomats get on with dealing with the world, whatever the consequences, and we get to live and enjoy our lives. It is a kind of exchange of irresponsibility or, more accurately, a pact between the unaccountable and the irresponsible. This may have made sense when the world was less integrated than now and when affairs of state touched only matters generally far removed from the affairs of ordinary people (and when democracy did not exist in any case). But today, when our lives are inextricably connected to the lives of

the other inhabitants of the planet, it makes no sense. Instead this exchange of irresponsibility fortifies and underpins the damaging competitive model of international relations, to the ultimate detriment of all.

4. The way that the diplomatic élites and most commentators and writers still think about foreign affairs is one again inherited from earlier history. States are seen as discrete actors with interests which must be arbitrated and negotiated with other states, sometimes bilaterally, sometimes collectively or multilaterally. Although, particularly in Europe, it is unfashionable to say that states have "interests" (instead, they have "values" which they pursue), even in Europe the behaviour of states and the diplomats who represent them reflects the more old-fashioned way of thinking. Germany wants x, France wants y. Negotiation between them, and with others concerned, may produce agreement z. Statesmen, diplomats and the journalists who report on their doings all adopt this model of description and behaviour. "US secures good agreement at UN Security Council"; "UK humiliated at EU Brussels summit". It is as if the states are football teams playing in a tournament. Indeed, sometimes international meetings are reported in this way (particularly relevant for soccer-loving countries) — " UK 0; France 1" (not a result to gladden the heart of any British Prime Minister). Intrinsic to this way of thinking is the idea that competition lies at the heart of states' behaviour. Each state looks out for its own interests; harmony lies in a balance of interests, secured through negotiation and diplomatic communication. Where interests are in opposition, sometimes armed conflict must result. Self-interest is seen as the driving motor of international relations. It is of course an echo of contemporary economic ideology that the maximisation of welfare lies in the individual pursuit of self-interest. But just like that ideology, such a way of thinking about international relations produces flawed results which may have nothing to do with the collective (or even individual) interests of mankind.

5. This model may have been relevant for a time when the collective interests of mankind were rather less obvious than they are now. But at a time when global warming, resource shortage (whether of oil or water), disease (AIDS, bird flu), migration and non-state violence are the most urgent problems facing us as individuals and collectively, it is dangerously inappropriate. Our problems are collective; ergo, the solutions must be collective too. Unfortunately, however, the supranational institutions established to deal with these problems are not producing effective solutions to any of these problems. The reason is that they are not truly supranational institutions at all, and they reflect the same calculus of traditional international relations: that consensus is produced by the bargaining of states' interests to produce an acceptable agreement. Moreover, the mere existence of these institutions, with their institutional self-interest in claiming that they are effective, predisposes us to complacency about our collective problems: the pact of irresponsibility at work again.

6. Beneath these more institutional and structural problems lie more fundamental problems concerning the way that practitioners think about international relations and diplomacy, in other words what these practitioners regard as acceptable information and what they do not. There is a deep commitment to certain forms of information and a rejection of others. Dispassionately-presented factual information is taken as a superior form of information, and as "objective", when presentation of all information, including in such form, represents a choice about what is important to us and what is not, and thus brings into play our emotions, personal prejudices and intuitions. This is not to say that all information is equally valid, and that all truth is relative. But it is an odd and problematic deficit in the discourse of diplomacy that certain types of information should be so rigorously excluded. One specific deficit in discussion of international relations is the difference between description and reality. Decisions in foreign policy are invariably taken at several removes from the reality they are trying to affect or arbitrate. Thus such decisions must be based on descrip-

tions. Such descriptions are thus inevitably deficient, and may exclude the essence of what is going on in any particular situation. We need to find ways to account for the irrational, the ineffable and other vital elements of what makes us human and comprises our reality. Diplomacy should take a more eclectic approach to information, and allow discussion and examination of emotion and non-measurable elements of reality, and at the least acknowledge this deficit in its calculations.

7. Related to this is a kind of conceit: that the world is comprehensible at all. The world is now overwhelmingly complex (perhaps it always was so). It is incomprehensible if you rely on any singular theory of how states, or individuals, or indeed anything, behaves. Governments, states and diplomacy are premised on simplification: that the world's complexity can be described and put into an order about which we can then take decisions. Governments and politicians, and the diplomats who serve them, have a profound interest in claiming that they can understand and order the world in this way. They cannot be anything other than wrong. Simplification, though tempting, must inevitably be inaccurate and wrong and is therefore dangerous. Academics are as guilty of this thought-crime as the politicians, providing glib generalisations with which we can organise our thoughts and dinner-party arguments. The absurdity of theses such as "the clash of civilizations" or the "end of history" (though the latter book admits to a more nuanced analysis) is only revealed at the point that any situation, anywhere, is examined using such templates.

8. At a more prosaic level, contemporary diplomacy is deeply unbalanced and unfair. Its practice and machinery are dominated by rich and powerful states, whose political and economic power is reinforced and supplemented by their less-recognised diplomatic power. Big, rich and established countries have large cadres of experienced, well-trained and well-resourced diplomats who are able to dominate negotiations. They are better informed and more able to turn negotiations to their advantage (for instance, at the

UK Mission to the UN in New York, our lawyers frequently prepared the first draft of texts for negotiation whether as resolutions or statements; as any negotiator knows, this is a huge advantage). On the other side of the table, poorer and less experienced countries (and particularly non-state groups) often struggle to get their point of view heard, let alone accommodated. This is obviously disadvantageous to them but nor does it serve the powerful, although they may wrongly think so. For agreements that do not address the interests of all concerned, above all those affected, are not good agreements and they are unlikely to have the desired effects or to endure. Ways need to be found to enable all those affected to be heard and their interests somehow addressed. This is the "diplomatic deficit" that Independent Diplomat, the non-profit advisory group I founded in 2004, was designed to address.

All of these problems are mixed up in the confused and secretive discourse known as diplomacy and statecraft. The practitioners and analysts of this discourse love to pretend that it is complex and arcane,[4] the better to preserve its privileges and power for themselves. But the business of contemporary international affairs is everybody's business, because it affects us all.

Moreover, by erecting elaborate barriers to entry and sticking to irrelevant and outdated philosophies of international relations (which we examine later), the diplomats and statesmen have become very confused about the nature of diplomacy and international relations. Academics provide complicated theses about realism, liberalism, neo-realism and neo-conservatism, but overlook the fact that international relations is ultimately about simple effects on simple people: it is merely politics. In their endless struggle to define what their state wants, the diplomats have forgotten that their state, and our common world, is just people and the environment in which they live.

We need a much more critical and intrusive approach to the world of diplomacy and international affairs. The stuff at stake here is nothing less than our future and it is time we paid it some attention. And it is time too to consider abolishing the discourse of diplomacy altogether. The idea that statecraft and international relations form some separated practice that can be removed from other forms of politics and government, with its own separate rules and philosophies, is unjustified in an age where everything is connected.

There is a paradox here. In a world of ever more connected events and phenomena, there is a greater need to discuss than ever before our affairs with our fellow humans. We need more diplomacy! But this book questions whether diplomacy — at least in its current forms — is the best way to undertake this task. Abolishing the restrictions, simplifications, abstractions, inventions and arbitrariness of diplomacy may require abolishing the idea of diplomacy itself.

2

THE EMBASSY

Bonn 1992-95

My first full posting as a diplomat was to Germany and its then capital, Bonn. The British embassy in Bonn was an ugly concrete block on the main road connecting the city and its suburb, Bad Godesberg. Everything about it was grey — the carpets, the walls, the faces of the people working there. My office overlooked the often-rainswept car park. If I craned my neck, I could see the road beside the embassy where cars sped between Bonn and Bad Godesberg.

My title was Second Secretary (Political), a junior diplomat, an embassy workhorse. The embassy had a large staff of diplomats, whose work was divided into many sections. My job was to report on German foreign policy. To do this, I would get into my car or ride the tram to the Auswärtiges Amt, the German foreign ministry, or, occasionally, the Federal Chancellery (where the Chancellor and his staff had offices). Once there, I would walk the long corridors until I found the desk officer I was looking for and I would ask him what German policy was on country *x*. After taking a few notes I

would return to the embassy and compose a telegram or letter summarising what I had been told. That was it.

Once I had realised the essential simplicity of this task, I tried to make it more interesting. I would seek out Bundestag members to talk to; I would cultivate journalists. I even participated in training courses with young German diplomats. All the better to understand what was going on in German foreign policy, in theory; but in practice my motive was to escape the incredible boredom of my job. For the Foreign Office in London, known in the service simply as "London", was not in the least interested in the thoughts of the minor parliamentarians who were willing to talk to junior diplomats, and even less the insights of German journalists. They didn't want to understand Germany, they just wanted to know what it was doing. And indeed it is much more the job of embassies to do the understanding in order that their home countries will have a better sense of what the target country is doing. That's part of the point of embassies.

My beat was the world outside Europe. My friend J. covered "Europe", which in those days included the former Soviet Union but not Turkey (that was mine). German foreign policy in the rest of the world was, and still is, mostly routine: the pursuit of its "interests" in Asia, Africa and the Americas. Almost invariably, this meant trade. From Turkey to China, this was the abiding German interest. There was only one interest that came close in importance to trade: namely immigrants and how to stop them coming to Germany.

"London" was moderately interested in German Chinese policy (at least the department in London once replied to my letters). Trade with the Chinese rested largely on the degree of favour granted by the Chinese government, particularly in the case of large engineer-

ing contracts. So official visits to China, for example by Chancellor Kohl, involved lots of sycophancy to the government, the signature of large contracts (for new rail systems for instance), and a bit of lip-service to human rights. I was disproportionately curious about this last aspect, since this was what I thought most important about China, so I would always give it particular attention in my reports (usually to emphasise how little attention the Germans had given it in their exchanges with the Chinese). London was of course much more interested in the contracts and how little lip-service it too could get away with: indeed, I was told that the value of my reports was in helping London calibrate the British approach with that of the Germans.

I don't think that anyone I spoke to either in Bonn or in London was especially pleased that this was the manner and focus of our relationship with the Chinese. The German officials talked about it with a resigned air, that this was just the way things were. The desk officer for China in London and I, meanwhile, enjoyed an ironic to and fro, glossing over the "realpolitik" with humour. His true love was art. None of us really thought of questioning the direction of our policy. We just accepted that trade, not rights, should take priority. This was what foreign policy was about.

But the thing that most gripped the German government, which their officials would confess to me in quiet moments, was the risk that China would disintegrate (with a smack of pretence, they called it *centrifugalism*), launching a massive wave of immigrants towards Europe and above all, they feared, towards Germany. When I first heard it, this revelation astonished me since it had not occurred to me, nor did there seem much risk of it. But it made sense in the Germany of 1992, which that year had received nearly a million

asylum-seekers (*Asylanten*, as they were known derogatorily), most of them from Eastern Europe and, above all, from the disintegrating states of the Balkans.

My introduction to Germany was over a month of what is accurately called "immersion" with a family near Münster. For five suffocating weeks, I stayed with a German family in order to cement my language skills. My German certainly improved, and so did my understanding of Germans, at least some of them. Night after night on the television news, we would watch pictures of traumatised Bosnian refugees escaping the war(s). On one occasion a train filled with refugees had been stuck on one of Germany's eastern borders. The people on board had been trapped on the train for days and were very clearly in desperation and agony, their faces an unpleasant echo of earlier genocidal wars. One of my hosts turned to the other, "More bloody (*verdammte*) *Asylanten* coming to take our money." My days would be filled with what were supposed to be German lessons, which in a way they were: didactic lectures from the father on how unfairly Germany had been treated (there were war crimes on both sides during the war etc.). Every evening, the mother would return from her medical practice to regale us with incessant complaints about the appalling and untrustworthy behaviour of the Bosnian girl whom she had foolishly employed. To escape, I smoked in the garden (to enormous disapproval) and taught myself to juggle.

But in some ways that family was more connected to the reality of what was going on in the Balkans than we were in Bonn. At least they had some contact with real Bosnians. In Bonn, like all the other diplomats in the embassy, I had quickly to learn to defend British policy over the break-up of Yugoslavia from the criticisms of many

German officials and journalists. At that time (in the early 1990s), and indeed throughout the war, the "British" view, which was in fact the view of a few ministers and key officials, but which we were all required to uphold, was that the Yugoslav wars were a civil war, driven by ethnic hatreds. Unwilling to intervene to stop it, we presented the murderous killing as inevitable and unpreventable. All we could do in such circumstances, we argued, was provide humanitarian aid (which British troops, as part of UNPROFOR, bravely and professionally did) and prevent any inflow of arms through an embargo.

I did not understand the Balkans. But this did not prevent me or anyone else in the embassy from repeating the analysis set out above. Indeed, that is what we were told to do. On the war in former Yugoslavia, as on any controversial issue, "London" would send out regular "lines-to-take", setting out in succinct and well-crafted bullet points what "we" thought. I would read these, learn them and deploy them authoritatively whenever a German interlocutor would argue that we were standing by while genocide was perpetrated, or that we were preventing the Bosniaks from defending themselves by denying them arms. I believed those lines-to-take, which helped when I had to use them. I did not stop believing them until I actually went to Bosnia many years later.

If the lines-to-take failed to do the trick, as they usually did, we would resort to criticising the Germans or the Americans. For of course the Germans, claiming that their constitution did not allow it (which it then did not), were unable to intervene to stop the Serbs. And the Americans, well, that's a story better told by others.[1] It is human nature that when you are on weak ground you seek to undermine your attacker, rather than examine the ground on which you are standing. Once a position has been taken on an issue — for

example that the wars in Yugoslavia were a "civil war" — all analysis becomes suborned to that meta-analysis. Groupthink, in this case as in others, not only ruled but was encouraged. If we believed in a nice, tidy, ordered world of states, as British officials most emphatically did, then the break-up of a state was a Bad Thing and must be "contained". British policy seemed logical, and the facts could, if we chose, be made to fit our views (telegrams from our posts in the region, particularly Belgrade,[2] did just that). If you see one group fighting another inside the borders of a state and you believe in the primacy of the state as the organising unit of "international affairs", you will tend to see that conflict as a "civil war". You can disregard the now undeniable fact that this war was deliberately initiated by one group against another, where the first group used the extant machinery of government, in particular the army, to remove and often annihilate the other. That we may have been entirely wrong never seemed to occur to us. To this day you may still meet senior British officials who will repeat the "civil war, ancient ethnic hatreds" analysis, Srebrenica notwithstanding. Charge them with our inaction and they will, with knee-jerk certainty, immediately blame the Americans (for not bombing sooner) or the Germans (for recognising Croatia too soon) and usually both. In extreme cases they will even blame the Bosniaks, presumably for somehow instigating their own annihilation. Not for a moment will they concede that "we" might have been wrong.

My area of responsibility covered other, even bloodier events. One day (and only once) I was asked by London to find out what "Germany" thought about the killings in Rwanda. Following a routine explanation from the Auswärtiges Amt desk officer on why the killings were inevitable and impossible to prevent — and of course

I understood, he added, that Germany itself could not possibly do anything thanks to its constitutional position — I was treated to the desk officer's own more personal analysis of why the killing was so widespread. You see, he said, there's just not enough room for all of them in that little country (he asked condescendingly if I had been to Rwanda) and they must kill each other like rats in a cage.

Despite the fact that the worst killing in Europe since the Second World War was going on just a couple of hours' flight from where we sat, the war in ex-Yugoslavia impinged little on our conscious-nesses (Rwanda was barely spoken of). Both the British and German governments were much more preoccupied with "Europe" or rather the European Union, and the tedious battles over things like Quali-fied Majority Voting on milk packaging directives. The embassy had an entire team to cover such crucial questions.

Despite its sometimes vivid but abstract content of genocide and human rights, the day-to-day reality of my life in Bonn was dull be-yond words. Not for nothing did John le Carré, who once served in the embassy, describe the town as "half the size of Chicago cemetery and twice as dead". I acted in a couple of local amateur dramatic productions (don't ask). Occasionally I would drive very fast along the autobahn to Cologne, there to seek excitement (I didn't find any). I kept a diary, detailing the agonised, spasmodic but seemingly inevitable collapse of my relationship with my girlfriend who had stayed in London. I had a few friends in Bonn who, in the manner of those who become friends in dismal circumstances, were good ones. But my days were grey and lonely, all in all.

Recognising the limits of my official duties and perhaps, though he did not mention it, my melancholic aspect, my boss, an enlightened soul, encouraged me to pursue what I thought interesting. This was

an unusual attitude for a Foreign Office manager but he was and is a singular man. I decided to investigate the minorities in Germany, the outsiders. Working on and off as my regular duties allowed, I spent months on the task and eventually produced a weighty paper which I proudly despatched to London. Perhaps it was the Münster family who had inspired me, but I was fascinated by the many millions of people who lived in Germany but were not Germans, and in particular by those who lived there for many generations but were still not considered Germans, culturally if not legally. German residence law has since changed, but at that time, over six million "foreigners" were living in Germany without citizenship.

I will not repeat the contents of the paper, much as I enjoyed preparing and writing it. Its significance to my story is this. My researches led me to some of the most oppressed people in Germany, and perhaps in Europe (with the exception of the Balkans), at that time. The Roma and Sinti peoples (almost universally known in Germany as *Zigeuner*, or gypsies, the English word does not have the same derogatory overtones as the German) were, and I suspect still are, routinely discriminated against. I visited a community in what could only be described as a ghetto, for it was a dilapidated housing estate, set in an industrial zone on the outskirts of Hamburg. The chemical pollution from surrounding factories was so bad that the local council would not allow "ordinary" housing, but this was where the Roma had been housed. The estate was surrounded by barbed wire, with a kind of sentry box, occupied by a policeman, at the entrance. The conditions inside the estate — the dirt and overcrowding — were disgusting. The local Roma leader told me that ambulances would not attend emergency calls at the estate. The inhabitants were barred from all the local shops.

But the relevance of this depressing story is that this was the most potent and moving experience of my time in Germany. I was shocked. I tried to convey the experience in my paper back to London, but could not. Neither by employing a sub-Orwellian journalese nor the drier vocabulary of a diplomatic dispatch could I capture the full power of what I had seen. I developed, with my boss's help, a theory of minorities in Germany,[3] partly because I sought an order, an explanatory system, to understand the messy human reality I had witnessed and also in order to find terms (words like citizenship, identity and rights) more palatable to the discourse of diplomacy, where of course abstractions are much more comfortably consumed than cruder, more coloured representations of reality. It is simply not done to write to London that people are being screwed in Hamburg, Bosnia or anywhere else.

Moreover, since the condition of the Roma and indeed other minorities in Germany did not fall under the rubric of Britain's "interests" there, the report was not placed on the normal channels of the embassy's communication with "London", namely the classified and encrypted telegrams that would be circulated on receipt to officials across Whitehall in many different government offices. It was instead sent back in the "bag". This was our weekly diplomatic bag to London, which contained everything deemed least urgent, a means of transportation almost guaranteed to deter the recipient from reading the contents. Unlike the telegrams copied in their hundreds to numerous departments in the government, it was sent in a single envelope to the Germany Desk Officer in what was then known as the Western European Department. I never received a reply, or even an acknowledgement of receipt. Nor did I really expect one, because such matters are not really what foreign policy, and the Bonn

embassy, was "about", namely the hard stuff like EU governance, the future of NATO, trade negotiations and what "we" couldn't do about Bosnia. It was certainly not our business to comment on the internal affairs of an ally (we only do that to poor countries). The desperate condition of an oppressed minority was regarded, even by me, almost as a hobby, a thing apart from the core.

Afghanistan, Spring 2002

A thundering C-130 Hercules is swooping through the mountains. Just behind the pilots, I clamber on to a small platform and poke my head up into a small, perspex dome just large enough to accommodate my shoulders.

Pure exhilaration. I look out from the top of the fuselage with a panoramic view of the aircraft, to the rear its fin cutting through the wispy cloud, to either side its huge, stolid wings and bellowing engines. I turn forwards, and we break through the clouds, skipping sharp mountain peaks and diving steeply over an immense plain. It is like the dangerous pleasure of a child sticking his head through the sun-roof of a speeding car, but this is a huge aircraft and we are five thousand feet above the ground, roaring over the Hindu Kush, diving down towards Bagram.

Afghanistan. It was perhaps appropriate that this should be my last diplomatic posting, a brief sojourn from my permanent post in New York. As a teenager I had stuck a collection of postcards to the wall by my bed. One, a well-known photograph, showed a mujahideen fighter kneeling on a prayer mat in the Afghan mountains, his hands raised in supplication to Allah, a Kalashnikov by his side. Eric Newby's *A Short Walk in the Hindu Kush* had been one of my favourite

books; Ahmed Shah Masood's romantic struggle against the helicopter gunships and bombers of the Soviet Union my favourite war.

I had lobbied hard to be posted to Kabul when Britain reopened its embassy after the Taliban fell. My qualifications were scant: that I had "done" Afghanistan on the UN Security Council, for instance by negotiating the Security Council mandate for the International Security Assistance Force which now helped police Kabul. But only a very few British diplomats had even set foot in Afghanistan in the long years since the Soviet invasion. Fewer still knew anything of the local languages. And so it was that in March 2002 I found myself in the embassy, being served tea in the garden by the ancient retainer, who had loyally tended the gardens and buildings throughout Britain's long absence.

The former British embassy was now a ruin, a once grand but now decaying neo-classical ambassadorial residence set in a large estate littered with the burnt-out houses of the lower-ranking diplomats, their style that of suburban Surrey — mock Tudor in the Afghan hills, a home from home for the archetypal Bromley man of the British civil service. But the embassy site now belonged to Pakistan, and Britain was obliged to occupy a small corner of its former estate, a gathering of cramped, low-rise buildings which had once housed the embassy hospital.

The embassy team — the ambassador, the diplomats, the support staff and the many soldiers who protected us — shared a few small rooms. Our main office was a tiny drawing room and the corridor outside. We ate together in a long dining room, using the be-crested crockery and cutlery that the embassy's retainer had managed to save through the long years of Britain's absence (he had hidden the silver candlesticks too but these had been stolen, to his

great distress, by an early visitor from Britain's Special Air Service).
Bacon, eggs and cornflakes in the morning; beef and roast potatoes
for supper. Tea whenever you wanted it. The staff, cooped up in the
embassy for most of the time, talked of what they knew: the latest
soccer games in the Premiership, television soaps. In the evenings
we sometimes played games (Trivial Pursuit, charades) and drank
beer and whisky flown in at enormous expense by the Royal Air
Force. After four cosmopolitan years in New York, it felt like being
trapped in a rather stuffy hotel in Weymouth.

Afghanistan lurked behind the high walls that protected us from
"outside". The walls were topped with coils of razor wire and sack-
cloth netting, the latter to trap the rocket-propelled grenades that
were feared as the greatest threat to our safety. My job as the political officer in the embassy was to report to London on political
developments in the country. Before the posting, I had visions of
sitting in crowded tea-shops in Kabul chatting about politics with
the locals. Instead, on arriving, I learned that we were only allowed
beyond the walls of the embassy inside an armoured Land Rover
with an escort of at least two members of our close protection (CP)
team. Appointments had to be made days in advance in order to
allow the CP team to reconnoitre the site before our visit. This was
a frustrating and time-consuming process, involving endless failed
telephone calls to the few Kabulis who owned satellite phones or
sending out our local "fixer" to set up the meeting. Once the meeting was arranged and the reconnaissance complete, we would roll
up in our lumbering white Land Rover, the bodyguards would hop
out, machine guns at the ready, and I would emerge in my grey suit,
notebook in hand, interpreter at my side, bright-eyed and ready to
learn what was "really" going on in Afghanistan.

Naturally, this was not the best way to detect the complex and powerful forces sweeping that country. The Afghans I met were guardedly friendly, and with armed men at my side it was no surprise that they generally told me what we wanted to hear. They were pleased the Taliban had gone and grateful for our help (they were polite enough not to point out that the Talibs' defeat was largely the Americans' doing). They wanted peace, stability and — mentioned less often — democracy.

I spent a lot of my time talking to the impressive Afghans and UN staff who were working to prepare the *Loya Jirga*, the gathering of representative groups of Afghans from around the country that was to choose a new government ("democracy Afghan style" as some of my colleagues chose to call it). The UN, unencumbered by the stringent security precautions that so limited our work, was much better informed than we were, and moreover employed some of the more skilled and experienced Afghan "hands" in the international community (several were fluent in Pashtun and Dari). Desperate to get some kind of orientation in this unfamiliar country, I sought out all the factions I could identify on the political landscape and tried to talk to them all.

I made a few trips around the country to meet local leaders. When the Prime Minister's Special Representative visited Afghanistan, I accompanied him to call on the bear-like General Dostum in Mazar-i-Sharif and the delphic Ismail Khan in Herat. But my efforts to get out of Kabul on my own were thwarted by the fact that we could only travel by air (the roads were too dangerous) and then only in Royal Air Force planes (which were usually employed in more military duties) and once an escort of Royal Marines (to guard the aircraft and us on the ground on arrival) had been arranged. This I managed only

once, by goading a reluctant member of the British military to allow me to piggy-back on his own visit to the beautiful and remote town of Bamiyan (site of the famously destroyed Buddhas).

High in the mountains, we rode four-wheel drives bouncing down dirt tracks and steep valleys, then sat for hours, cross-legged, at a feast of lamb and rice discussing the future of Afghanistan with Karim Khalili, the leader of the Hazara sect:

Me (through interpreter): "Tell me, Mr Khalili, what do you think are the prospects for the *Loya Jirga?*"

To get home, our squad unfurled a small parabolic antenna on the roof of their Landcruiser and called down our C-130 to Bamiyan's dirt airstrip, where it barrelled in, roaring and spitting gravel from its wheels.

The mountains were very beautiful; the people picturesque. The light had a wonderful, limpid quality. But whether these images had much, or anything, to do with the real Afghanistan, remains a mystery to me. I spoke no local languages (there was only one person in the embassy — the interpreter — who did). All my conversations were thus limited to stilted, somewhat impersonal exchanges. The most resonant image of my time there is looking out at the people of Kabul, bustling and alive, through the cold, thick armoured glass of the CP Land Rover.

However, this separation did not prevent me from writing nice, clear telegrams (divided, as the Foreign Office practice dictated, into Summary, Detail and Comment) informing "London" what was going on in Afghanistan. My missives covered such diverse topics as the prospects for the *Loya Jirga*, the future of the Hazaras, and the celebrations in Kabul for the New Year (Nawruz) festival. I tried

to say that I didn't really know what was going on (I repeatedly mentioned the restrictions on our work, linguistic and otherwise), but I was being paid to produce a product, and produce it I did. And I did feel that there was one message that was worth getting across. This was the one thing that every Afghan I met, with the exception of the so-called warlords themselves (Dostum, Ishmail Khan *et al.*), told me and this was that they wanted to be free of the warlords. They wanted "security".

The UN said it too, the US Ambassador said it, as did mine, so did the military men I met from our own forces, and so did all the journalists. My own confinement to Kabul and protection by the CP team carried the same message. The country was not safe. ISAF provided a modicum of security in Kabul but outside it there was considerable anarchy, only moderated in limited areas by the auto-cratic and occasionally tyrannical rule of the regional big men, such as Dostum and Ismail Khan. Most striking of all were the messages carried to the organisers of the *Loya Jirga* by innumerable delega-tions from the regions: they wanted security; and they wanted ISAF deployed across the whole country to provide it. And although this of course was the one thing that everyone decent and sensible there said very clearly, it was the one thing that "we" — the UK and US governments — were not prepared to give them.

What the campaign to overthrow the Taliban was about, of course, was not the Afghans' security but our own, as defined by us. The reason why the smiles of welcome on the Afghans' faces were not as warm as they might have been was that they knew perfectly well that, but for 9/11, Osama bin Laden and all the rest, they would still be languishing, forgotten, under the rule of the Taliban.

Our protestations, from the Prime Minister downwards, that we would not again forsake Afghanistan, were met with scepticism.

While I was at the embassy, I slowly became aware that there was a different narrative being played out by the various powers in Afghanistan, one that hardly featured in the telegrams I or my Ambassador wrote, one that had nothing to do with building democracy, the *Loya Jirga* or anything so noble. [4]

After a while, I realised that while I was running around encouraging and cajoling politicians to engage in the *Loya Jirga* process, the purpose of which was in part to take power back from the warlords, others were running around doling out bribes to buy loyalty amongst those very same warlords. Their purpose, so they claimed, was to track down the terrorists, Al-Qaeda and the remnant Taliban or "AQT" as they were known. Although it took me a while to cotton on, this was and had been for some time an open secret among the international community in Kabul (in fact, I think it was someone from the UN who first told me about it). Indeed, it was something of a joke among the more cynical observers that the Afghans, within the government as well as the regional war-lords, were encouraging a bidding war between the foreign powers involved in Afghanistan — the US, UK, Russia, Pakistan and Iran, to start with — to extract the most cash. It was widely believed that some in the government were taking money from all of them (and who could blame them?).

It is not hard to see the contradictions. In the embassy, our version of reality went like this: we favoured a process (the *Loya Jirga*) leading to a democracy based around a centralised system of government, with the centre supreme over the regions and people like that nice Mr Karzai (who happens fortunately to speak a language we

can understand) in charge of the whole thing. Our activities and our reports were thus directed towards this end. The UN too, which helped run the interim administration and the *Loya Jirga* process, was working towards this aim.[5]

But meanwhile a different strategy was being played out, often entirely unknown to us. In theory it was a complementary strategy, but what has happened since suggests otherwise. This was to buy off the support of the regional powerbrokers in order to win their co-operation in the war against the "AQT". A further goal was added, which reinforced the contradictions. Shortly after the Taliban fell, someone in the British government remembered that Afghanistan was the source of much of the heroin that ended up in Britain. So the plan was hatched to remove this supply at a stroke by paying the farmers in the poppy-growing areas (otherwise known as most of Afghanistan) to plough in that year's crops.

This occupied many of the staff of the embassy, and several officers were drafted in especially for the task. Vast amounts of cash were dished out to the various regional leaders to pay off "their" farmers to destroy their crops.

The result of these strategies soon became clear. In 2002, according to the UN Drug Control Programme, the heroin crop in Afghanistan was ten times bigger than it had been in 2001, when the country was for most of the time under Taliban control (the Taliban were, with some exceptions, largely hostile to drug production in areas under their control). Meanwhile, the process of political stabilisation has faltered, it seems because of two main factors: the persistent insecurity and instability outside Kabul and the continuing intransigence of the regional warlords in ceding real control to the central administration. Indeed, by 2006 some analysts were argu-

ing that the warlords, and the drug runners, were now running the central government: a narco-state was in the process of creation.

How the war against terrorism — "AQT" — is going I do not know, but over the four years since the allied invasion there have continued to be bloody skirmishes in the south and areas bordering Pakistan, where the remnant Taliban (if that is who they really are) are strongest. The signs, even in early 2002, soon after the Taliban had so precipitately collapsed, were inauspicious. Twice I visited Bagram airbase, where much of the British military were then stationed. A senior British officer there voiced his fear that the strategy that the allies (his polite way of indicating the Americans) were adopting would perpetuate the very problem it was designed to solve. He gave an example.

Aerial reconnaissance had photographed an encampment close to the Pakistan border which bore suspicious signs that it might be an AQT base. There appeared to be circular pits, perhaps for mortars or small artillery, camouflaged trucks and trenches. A British patrol was sent to investigate. First, it observed the camp from the hilltops above, but could not tell what was going on. So they boldly decided to descend to find out more. On entering the village, which it turned out to be, they realised that the settlement was not AQT but a camp of nomads, the Kuchi, as they are known in Afghanistan. The "gun pits" were circles made in the grass by goats tied to stakes. The "trenches" were drainage ditches and the "camouflaged trucks" were ragged old tents. The patrol was greeted with a friendly welcome, and they went on their way after arranging for an airdrop of "HR" (humanitarian relief).

Had "our allies" first received the information of this encampment, argued the officer, they would have bombed it flat. As he

spoke, A-10 Warthog ground attack aircraft taxied along the run-way behind him and blasted into the air for another mission. (The incidents of accidental bombings of civilians in Afghanistan have been frequent since then. For example, in May 2006 over a dozen civilians were reportedly killed when their village was struck by al-lied bombs.) The officer argued that the "allied" goal was to kill as many AQT as possible, not to win over the local population. At the same time, there were plenty of people, he argued, not only in Afghanistan but also from the surrounding countries, who were delighted to come to fight the Americans. Thus a cycle would be established and perpetuated.

In June 2006, over 22,000 US and British combat troops remain deployed in Afghanistan to fight the "AQT".

The thick screen of "armour plating" and bodyguards that separated us from the reality of Afghanistan was unusual, but in its way symp-tomatic of the separation of the embassy from its surroundings. It successfully allowed us to project our own narrative on to what was "really" going on, even if the consistent message from the Afghans who broke through our screen was a clear one.

What I experienced in Kabul and Bonn has echoes of other epi-sodes of diplomatic history. The then British ambassador candidly admitted the failure of his embassy in Tehran to detect the rum-blings of frustration and revolt which led to the overthrow of the Shah in 1979. We were distracted, he confessed. What the work of his embassy had been "about" was maximising sales to the friendly and pro-western Shah, whether of tanks or chemical plants.

Even in countries very similar to our own, like Germany, there is an inevitable tendency for the diplomat to gravitate towards those like us; those who speak our language, or share our values. For they are inevitably easier to find — indeed they may seek us out. They may become our friends (as the Shah and many of his ministers became of the British ambassador), and come to comprise our understanding and memory of what Germany, or Iran, or Afghanistan is.

(In Afghanistan, the diplomats, UN staffers, NGOs and journalists formed a large group of expatriates who socialised and gossiped together. It was too unsafe and, frankly, alien to socialise with the Afghans. The journalists looked to the diplomats for information, and we did the same to them. Thus a circle was formed, where we were able to confirm our chosen narratives of what was "really" going on. There were some great journalists and international workers who rejected the temptations of this circle of affirmation, and sought out the facts on their own, but they, regrettably, seemed to be the exception.)

The good diplomat will resist this tendency, but it is difficult, even for the most diligent. As the screen of security around US, British and other western embassies grows ever thicker, it will become even harder for the diplomat to locate and meet "real people": my dream of sitting in tea-houses in Kabul with "ordinary" Afghans remained a fantasy. It was easier for me to meet them in New York.

But this restriction will not prevent the embassy from producing detailed reports on what is going on in its host country, just as I dutifully reported from inside the fence in the embassy in Kabul. The local government will still speak to us from inside its fence and

thus the utility of embassies, government speaking to government, is in this narrow sense preserved.

Ambassadors and diplomats moreover tend to emphasise their intimate relations with the local authorities, as a mark of how well they are doing their job. When I was a diplomat, ambassadors took great care to relay to London detailed accounts of every mutter and hint of their late-night conversation or round of golf with the President or Prime Minister. Usually, these accounts would be given a high classification and restricted circulation, in order to underline the unusual access the diplomat has secured (even if the information contained is banal). They are often spiced with little personal details (the President's favourite whisky; his fondness for the British royal family etc.) in order to demonstrate the intimacy and uniqueness of the exchange. The product of such behaviour is to reinforce the sense that diplomacy offers a rarefied and unique level of communication, where one élite talks to another, elevated from the cacophonous hordes beneath.

This remains one service that embassies can perform for their governments.

3

THE NEGOTIATION (1)

UN Security Council, New York, 2001

W hat is a fact?
This was not a post-modern philosophical debate; it was a negotiation of what was to become international law. But this essential question bedevilled our discussion. We could not agree on the facts.

We were meeting day after day, for several hours at a time. Our discussions took place in a narrow, cramped room called the NAM caucus room. NAM is the acronym for the Non-Aligned Movement, the grouping of those states that during the Cold War saw themselves as associated with neither NATO nor the Warsaw Pact. Although the Cold War is over, the NAM lives on, as does its room, which is next to the room next to the UN Security Council (perhaps a situational reflection of the NAM's distant relationship to real power). The room is too small for the NAM, which has 116 members; indeed it is too small for the fifteen delegates of the members of the Security Council. The table only accommodated ten people, tightly squeezed together, so whoever entered the room last had

no seat at the table, and was forced to sit on the uncomfortable chairs behind, lining the wall. When the negotiations began, there would be an ungentlemanly rush for the table seats, and whoever was last in the room would have to spend the next several hours awkwardly balancing their negotiating papers on their knees. However, this problem did not last long. After the first few days, some of the smaller non-permanent[1] Council delegates stopped bothering to attend the negotiations at all, even though their countries would have to vote on the outcome.

It might seem cynical or even idle not to bother to attend negotiations on such an important subject as the future of sanctions on Iraq. But these were small delegations, heavily overloaded with the many agenda items on the Security Council, and the truth was that they were irrelevant. Some of the more competent non-permanent delegations were often able to make a meaningful contribution to Council negotiations, despite the limitations of their tiny size (they might have three or four overworked diplomats covering the entire agenda of the Council, where Britain, by contrast, had at least a dozen). But their role was really more that of spectators at the main fight. We all knew that they would vote for whatever outcome the permanent members could agree to, and they knew it too. So not bothering to attend was, in a sense, entirely rational on their part. It also meant that there was more room at the table.

Our negotiation was to agree the terms of what we called the "rollover" of the Oil-for-Food programme in Iraq. Every six months the terms of the programme had to be negotiated afresh in order for the Council to agree, by adopting a new resolution, to implement the programme. But although technically this was what the negotiation was about, the actual discussion was concerned with

how much or how little we were going to ease sanctions on Iraq, for the resolution on the Oil-for-Food programme also stipulated, in arcane yet often imprecise detail, what Iraq could and could not import or export, and how these flows were to be regulated.[2]

And this was why we couldn't agree the facts. By 2001, when this negotiation took place, the debate over sanctions on Iraq had calcified into two opposing and entirely incompatible views.

On the one side were us (the British) and the Americans, with perhaps one or two sympathetic non-permanent members, like the Dutch, and on the other everyone else, led by the French and, less articulately, by the Russians. The US/UK view was that sanctions were essential in the face of Iraq's non-compliance with its obligations to disarm of its Weapons of Mass Destruction.[3] If there was humanitarian suffering in Iraq, it was the fault of the Iraqi government for its failure to comply with its disarmament obligations and for failing to implement properly the Oil-for-Food programme, which since 1996 had existed to allow Iraq to purchase, through the UN, necessary humanitarian supplies, including all types of food and medicine.

To justify our argument we could deploy a whole array of "facts", for example that in northern Iraq, where the UN rather than the Iraqi government was in charge of running the programme, hospitals and schools were being set up and operated smoothly, and supplies were being successfully delivered to those who needed them (indeed, so successful was the Oil-for-Food programme in the north that the Kurdish parties would lobby us to make sure that it wouldn't be stopped if sanctions ever had to be lifted). Another fact consisted of the reports of the UN administrators of the programme, the Office of the Iraq Program, which suggested that it was delivering

humanitarian improvements. In addition, a routine argument used by our politicians was the fact that Saddam was building and furnishing lavish palaces while his people were suffering (we tended not to use this argument in negotiation; somehow it seemed too crude and propagandist, something we diplomats were supposed to be above). We could cite import orders, placed through the UN (as all import orders, legal ones at least, had to be) for ludicrously unnecessary goods, like 10,000 tons (yes, tons) of neckties or 25,000 musical doorbells. Cigarettes and whisky were being imported by the regime in vast quantities. All of this meant that it was all the fault of the government of Iraq, not of sanctions, if people were suffering.

On the other side, the opponents of sanctions had assembled an equally devastating array of "facts". They cited evidence of hospitals without medicines, undernourished children, schools with neither books nor desks, sewage systems without spare parts, power stations that didn't work, ambulances without tyres. They could trot out one report after another, some from NGOs, some from the Iraqi government (which surpassed itself in the hysterical language it used to describe the suffering of the Iraqi people) and some from the UN. Most famously, there was a UNICEF report which, projecting from mortality data from before the first Gulf War, estimated that some 500,000 children had died in the period since sanctions were first imposed, deaths that would not have occurred if pre-sanctions mortality rates had remained stable. This rather complicated and measured judgement had been spun by opponents of sanctions into the statement that sanctions had killed half a million Iraqi children, which, UNICEF would say, was an oversimplification of their conclusion (even if it might nevertheless be true). And simplification

begets exaggeration, as Osama bin Laden was later to say that sanctions had killed two million Iraqi children.

To each and every fact on either side of the argument, we developed counter-facts. When others raised the UNICEF report, we would politely nod and say something like: yes, that's a serious figure but (cue frown) it is based on Iraqi government figures — which it was — and (suck teeth) I'm afraid we cannot treat those as reliable. And to every one of our arguments, the French and Russians deployed their own battery of rebuttals. They would argue, for instance, that the northern provinces of Iraq received a disproportionately large share of the proceeds from the Oil-for-Food programme (which was true, although the disproportion was not enough to explain the difference in welfare in the north). The egregious examples of Iraqi government wastage and inefficiency did not show that sanctions should continue in their current form, etc. On both sides there were skilled diplomats who spent their time scouring UN reports and writing briefs, dedicating their intelligence and energy to rubbishing one another. If the negotiations became stuck, as they always did, at the level of the delegates or "experts",[4] as they are known in the insider language of the Security Council, we would organise a round of negotiation at ambassador level. There exactly the same arguments would be repeated, except by different people and with more or less fluency, depending on the individual — the Russian ambassador, for instance, was not only a brilliant and lucid advocate in English, but also had a thorough familiarity with the arguments. The only other significant difference was that the ambassadorial discussion would take place in another room, this time the "informal" Security Council chamber.

The result, needless to say, was total deadlock. Negotiation became a tedious recitation of their "facts" and our "facts", thrown to and fro across the table. We only persisted in this trench warfare because each of us was trying to convince the non-permanent members that we were right, in the hope that this would convince them later to vote for this or that proposal in the resolution. This too was largely a waste of time since they knew that any of the permanent members could block any proposal they didn't like, and in any case the crossfire of arguments soon made the debate unintelligible. It got so bad that we would reject anything the French and Russians proposed simply because it was *their* proposal, and vice versa. Indeed, on several occasions we would introduce a new proposal (say, to modify some aspect of the process to screen exports to Iraq) only to have it opposed without concession by the other side. Then, six months later, come the next "rollover" debate, they would propose exactly the same idea, only this time we would oppose it, because we couldn't believe that there wasn't some hidden catch which would allow the Iraqi regime and their allies a loophole.

You will notice one major absentee in this discussion: the Iraqi people themselves. As we irritably traded arguments in the NAM caucus room, ordinary Iraqis were struggling with a defunct economy, eking out their dwindling incomes and coping. It is all too easy to see now how their fates could become a debating point in a fetid negotiation chamber. What we all lacked in that nasty overheated little room was any sense of what was really going on. Almost every source of information was in some way compromised and thus could be dismissed by one side or the other. For the British and Americans we could always deploy one argument if all others failed, and this was that *any* report coming out of Iraq was inevitably questionable

since organisations could only operate there under the supervision of the Iraqi government. Even the UN itself could not be impartial: we suspected some agencies of becoming "politicised" (as if everything was not already politicised in this debate), led by people with an "agenda". Other agencies were less suspect, and it was their reports that we tended to quote. Thus observers of the debate were treated to the absurd spectacle of each side quoting supposedly impartial UN reports at one another — and, as Germaine Greer once said, "all quotations are taken out of context: that's what they are."[5] All our information was out of context.

However, I should not play this "he says, she says" point too far. The absence of good, hard, reliable data and our own skill at demolishing our opponents' arguments helped us avoid a very important truth, perhaps even The Truth. There may not have been good facts, but that should not have prevented us from seeing the obvious. After several rounds of this type of discussion, I began to find it deeply disturbing. There is something very wrong about sitting around a table in New York arguing about how many children are dying in Iraq and whose fault it was. By 2001 I had been doing the job for over three years. I had met a large number of UN staffers and NGO workers, as well as many diplomats from other countries who were present in Iraq (neither we nor the Americans had had diplomatic relations and thus embassies in Baghdad since the invasion of Kuwait), and even the occasional "real" (i.e. non-government) Iraqi. These were not people with an "agenda". And they all agreed on one point. Things were bad and had been bad for a long time. I slowly realised, as I should have done long before, that it was much more important to do what we could to ameliorate the situation than to expend our energies attributing blame for it.

This realisation had begun slowly to filter into the British government more generally. The lobby against sanctions in Britain was considerably more vociferous and well-organised than in the US (perhaps simply because of proximity). Our ministers were finding it increasingly hard to justify sanctions in the face of pictures of children dying for lack of necessary drugs or overflowing sewage systems (they were not as practised as the diplomats were in firing off the barrage of counter arguments, tending instead to rely on the weaker forms of generalised propaganda — palaces and whisky again). A polemical film against sanctions by John Pilger had made a particular impact (it was never shown on general release in the US). And so the government decided to review its policy.

A policy review sounds grand, but it is not. The term conjures up images of learned mandarins bent over reams of documents, scrutinising, examining, weighing up the options. When we at the Mission were told there would be a review, I imagined thoughtful missives bouncing around between embassies and the Foreign Office, ministers, experts, civil servants all joined together in a common endeavour, the select, the policymakers. We were clever, we were concerned, we would get it right. I was wrong.

The review began in early 1999 and it was not complete until the next year. It consisted largely of a desultory exchange of ill-informed letters from senior officials. Most of them were so ignorant of the existing measures that they would propose changes that had long ago been introduced. All of our views, including mine, were uninhibited by any connection with empirical reality on the ground. One official, from the Ministry of Defence, opined in strong terms that since sanctions would "never work", the only recourse was military action (my colleagues and I at the mission thought this laughable

at the time, little realising what was later to follow). Contributions
from our embassies in the region were facile, "The [insert name of
Arab population] will welcome some easing of sanctions, as there is
considerable concern on the street[6] at their humanitarian impact."
And, this being government, the review was secret. We might mutter to a few other diplomats that we were "having a think" about
sanctions, but the large number of NGOs and concerned individuals
— humanitarian experts, academics — who had taken an interest
in this controversial issue were ignored, unless we the officials happened to bother to read their reports, which most of us didn't. We
were too busy.

Part of the problem was that sanctions policy was so complex that
only a very few people understood it. At the Mission, most of our
contributions to the review consisted of correcting the misunder-
standings of other senior officials. Only when a particular individual
was put in charge of the whole review did any coherence start to
emerge. He took the trouble to spend some time on the subject, and
learn some of its intricacies. Whenever ministers became involved,
the debate would have to be reduced to such a level of simplicity that
all meaning was removed. One particular minister would occasionally touch on the subject with his American opposite number. The
records would show that a few generalities would be exchanged,
"yes, I agree we need a rethink, better focus, that kind of thing".
Then the conversation would move on to more exciting topics, with
the details, as ever, "left for the officials". The trouble was that the
details *were* the policy. Only once, much later, in this long process
did one minister — to his great credit — bother to get to grips with
the detail. We were in the thick of trying to persuade the Russian
foreign minister to accept what had become our new revised sanc-

tions proposal. At his request, I wrote the minister a 20-page brief on the topic. He read it that night and the next day deployed it to devastating effect. Ivanov appeared completely stunned.

After several tortuous months of the review, we managed to agree inside the Foreign Office on what we should do. The summary of the idea was simple: the present situation was that Iraq was not allowed to import anything except those goods which were explicitly approved by the UN Sanctions Committee. Now, we would allow Iraq to import anything except those items which were explicitly prohibited. A sort of reversal. The concept was neat — good for soundbites — but the details were complicated and difficult. Moreover, before we could even begin to persuade the Security Council to adopt the new system, we had to persuade the Americans. This was to prove much harder than we anticipated, because the State Department, unlike the British government, was under no political pressure to alter sanctions at all. On the contrary, they were worried that any new system would be condemned by the Republican right as "going soft" on Saddam (this was during the last days of the Clinton administration). The complexity of the policy also meant that our ministers were rarely able to exert any leverage in their contacts with the Americans (leaving it to the officials, invariably). However, long sessions at "State" (as we insiders call it) and endless cajoling telegrams to get "London" to pressure "Washington" eventually had their effect.

And so, with the Americans somewhat reluctantly on board, we went to the Security Council and proposed our new measure, soon to be characterised by the press, though never by us, as "smart sanctions" (inviting the obvious retort, from Iraq's Deputy Prime minister Tariq Aziz, that previous sanctions had been "stupid").

And thus it was that I found myself chairing a meeting of the Security Council "experts" to try to get them to agree to it. (Since it
was our proposal, we had taken it upon ourselves to convene and
chair the meetings.)

It was at first a thrill to negotiate international law for one's
country. When I first did it, at the beginning of my tour in New
York, I would bound out of bed every morning at the excitement
of the prospect. I remember being so thrilled that I whooped to
myself in the shower: wow, this was the business, the hard core.
But by the time we came to negotiate "smart sanctions" (we soon
wearily accepted the name; everyone else was using it), I was a little
more jaded. This was my seventh "rollover" of the Oil-for-Food
programme. Most of the "experts" had changed, but the arguments
had remained the same. Indeed, it felt as if I was stuck in an unfunny
diplomatic version of *"Groundhog Day"* with the same episode being replayed over and over again. You say "civilian deprivation"; I
say "Iraqi non-cooperation". Fresh ideas were hard to come by, and
even when they appeared, they were invariably rejected. This new
initiative — smart sanctions — was fresher and better than most,
but our clever new weapon failed to alter the nature of the war
— we were back in the trenches, hurling the same old canards, and
I was still stuck in that same horrid airless NAM caucus room.

This time round the atmosphere was particularly bad. Years of
argument had entrenched deep animosities among the "experts".
National differences had become personal feuds. When the American delegate spoke, the French would stare at the ceiling and smirk.
When the French had their turn, the Americans would shuffle their
papers and whisper to one another. It was unpleasant to be in that

room. And it became clear, soon after we began, that we would be stuck there for a very long time.

The Americans felt that since they were offering such a massive new concession, everyone should gratefully accept it without question. The French and Russians, unaccustomed to such flexibility, were exaggeratedly suspicious, querying every tiny detail for fear that we were deceitfully introducing some new and unwarranted means of control. Meanwhile, the Iraqi government hated the new scheme, realising that if it worked as we hoped, it would remove once and for all the humanitarian argument to lift sanctions. To what extent their opposition to the initiative played a part in French and Russian hostility, I do not know and only those governments could answer (and they will not do so), but the fact that the Iraqi government was so implacably against the scheme did nothing to help our cause, whatever the cynicism lying behind their reasons. All this produced the ingredients for yet another nasty, slow and unproductive negotiation.

After the talks began late one week, I returned to London to attend the wedding of an old friend. The event was a respite from my dessicating work in New York and the singing of the choir uplifted me. On the flight back to New York, an idea occurred to me. The following Monday, my colleague and I took a portable music player into the NAM caucus room. I made a suggestion. Why didn't we take it in turns to play a song at the beginning of each session?

I turned to my colleague, and he turned on a CD from the British singer, formerly of The Jam, Paul Weller:

> *Day by day*
> *Going, just where I'm going*

Getting to where
We should be going

The delegates would usually fidget and chatter at the beginning of each session. It would take several minutes for people to settle down and work, and longer still for them to listen to each other. This time it was different. Silence fell as the song began; a sense of tranquillity spread among us. I caught the eye of the Bangladeshi delegate and he smiled. After the song, I asked G. to explain why he had chosen it and why he liked it. The other delegates listened quietly. And, when we began our discussions, going line-by-line through the draft resolution we had proposed, the rancour and acidulous tone of earlier sessions had disappeared. The differences of substance were still as acute, but the acrimony had passed. The next day the Chinese delegate brought in a beautiful, haunting tune from medieval China relating, he told us, the last moments of a doomed general as he faced his enemy. The day after that, the Bangladeshi brought in a love song, sung by a shepherd in the vast delta at the heart of that country, a song of unrequited love.

And so the negotiations proceeded. One afternoon, the Reuters correspondent at the UN telephoned me at the mission. She had seen us carrying the music player into the NAM caucus room. The French delegate had told her what it was for. She asked me to confirm the story and, since there was no point in denying it, I did. She ran the story, and from there, things began to get out of hand. Just as our own discussions bore precious little relation to the realities of life in Iraq, the representations of our music initiative had even scantier connection to what was going on in that little room. The BBC got hold of the story and managed to interview Paul Weller about the use of his song. Generously, he said he was pleased and

that it was somehow appropriate that we had used his song to calm
hostilities because it was about love. They also interviewed a professor of music, who was intrigued that we had chosen non-linguistic negotiating techniques. The British press began to run the
story, as did some of the US press. Then the Iraqi ambassador was
interviewed about it and expressed his outrage that we were trivi-
alising the fate of his people. Inspired perhaps by this, the Tunisian
ambassador raised a complaint in a formal session of the Security
Council (his delegate in the room had told me he had enjoyed the
music and was busy planning his own song). We had to stop. But
the story did not need our music to keep running. It now circled
the world with articles in Europe, Asia and, above all, the Middle
East. An anti-sanctions campaigner wrote to a mass-market British newspaper saying that I was a disgrace to the British foreign
service.

It was uncomfortable for once to be the object rather than the
subject. Diplomats, particularly British ones who speak with a
comfortable anonymity ("British diplomats said", "Western officials
commented"), are used to privacy. Only rarely do we find ourselves
in the ungenerous light of publicity. At first, I enjoyed the attention
and felt rather clever and pleased with myself (a German diplomat
approached me in the corridors of the UN and said it was the coolest
thing he'd ever heard of). As the commentary turned more critical,
I naturally liked it less and I began to realise how our actions would
be seen. We were used to carrying on in private — now for once,
our machinations were public and it became clear that the world,
when it saw what we were up to, would not be wholly approving. The music in the Security Council became a Rorschach test
for the Iraqi sanctions debate. In the US press, and mostly in the

British press too, in such comment as there was, this was an amusing, somewhat curious little incident.[7] In the Arab press, our music was seen as yet another example of the crass inhumanity of western diplomats, dancing on the graves of Iraqi children.

The negotiations moved on to the deadline of the end of that six-month span of the Oil-for-Food programme. Music notwithstanding, we failed to overcome the objections of the Russians (the French came around sooner): there were more questions over the contents of the lists of prohibited items than there was time to resolve, and for months to come the US was mired in highly complex negotiations over the specifications of prohibited goods.[8] Iraqi resistance remained intractable. Our smart sanctions would have to wait for the next rollover six months later, when they were at last agreed. G. was in charge of the negotiations this time: I had volunteered to serve a brief spell in our embassy in Kabul. There was no music, just G's quiet professionalism to guide the negotiations. And they managed to agree. But by then Washington was well on its way to deciding an altogether different course, and smart sanctions was no longer seen as the necessary redeemer of a bad policy.

Sanctions on Iraq were inhumane and I was intimately involved in both their maintenance and their design. Many people suffered as a result of our misconceived policy. Somehow, in our creation of two irreconcilable narratives of what was "really" going on, reality — at least that of the Iraqi people — got lost. How did this happen?

A traditional analysis would portray this episode as a tale of an inevitable collision of the irreconcilable interests of nation states sitting on the Council. US interests were to maintain sanctions (despite the later claims of the US and UK governments, our internal

assessments were that sanctions were highly effective in preventing significant rearmament by Iraq). British interests were to ameliorate the effects of sanctions in order to improve their international acceptability, and thus to maintain them. The Russians and French would say that their interest was to make sure that our new sanctions initiative did not in fact make matters worse for the Iraqi population (there were indeed some grounds for supposing that the elaborate new system we had designed would, at least initially, make it more complicated to export goods to Iraq). But both of course had substantial economic interests at stake too: the Iraqi regime had signed contracts with a number of Russian, French and Chinese oil companies for the exploitation of Iraq's enormous reserves when sanctions were lifted.

Put more critically, all of us were failing in our responsibility under the UN charter to maximise security and minimise suffering. Russian and French intransigence no doubt gave great comfort to the Iraqi government in its campaign to resist cooperation with the Security Council. I have little hesitation in saying this: Iraqi diplomats would tell me so, as they crowed that sanctions were crumbling and it was we, the UK and the US, who were isolated in the world, not them. Meanwhile, I have equally little doubt that, for our part, although we may not have had legal responsibility for the welfare of the Iraqi people, we had a moral responsibility. We should have done a lot more a lot sooner to reduce the unquestionably harmful effects of sanctions. It would be too easy to blame this on the Americans, and indeed they were even less inclined to ease sanctions than the British were, but we could have done more, a lot more. There were good alternatives, which were never properly pursued.[9]

Another form of analysis would see this as a story of bad group dynamics, with young to middle-aged people, mostly men, arguing and not listening, refusing to accord to one another even the possibility that they might be right. And indeed there was something ugly going on in that group. Petty rivalries and animosities were allowed to influence debate on a much larger issue. To my shame I remember the pleasure I felt at my little triumphs, such as when the UK draft resolution became the only draft under discussion and the rival French draft fell away, irrelevant and defeated like a vanquished knight (not for nothing is the entrance to the British ambassador's residence in New York lined with prints of Waterloo). We would whine to our ambassador when the French had been particularly rude, and, like a good Dad, he would ring up the French ambassador to admonish him. It was more than a little childish.

But there was something else going on too, something that my account may have made clear to the reader but did not become clear to me until long after I left the mission. We believed that we were dealing with real facts and real people. We had a positive belief in information. Our information was good; our opponents' was biased. And of course they believed the opposite. One of us must have been wrong.

If, instead of playing music, we could have transported ourselves to the ward of a children's hospital in Saddam city, a slum of Baghdad, or to a school; if we could have spent six months in Iraq instead of six months in negotiation, then things might have been different. I suspect — I do not know, and never will — that our arguments would have subsided and we would have sought instead to find practical ways to do something. My colleagues and I spent many hours dreaming up schemes to try to improve conditions in Iraq

(history will not long remember the "cash component", a scheme to allow the UN to fund projects with direct cash locally, rather than having to import all goods through the Oil-for-Food programme). None of them came to anything. When we proposed them, they were blocked. When our opponents advocated similar ideas, we were truculent. We once proposed a visit by a team of "objective" UN-appointed experts (real experts this time, not the diplomats): although we managed to get the Council to agree the initiative, the Iraqi government refused to allow them in. I even applied to visit myself in order to see with my own eyes (one's own eyes of course being entirely reliable witnesses of the "truth"): the Iraqi government denied my visa application. Absent any encounter with reality, we worked in a futile abstraction.

Of course all information, whoever mediates it, is something less than what it is describing. No amount of statistics can convey the bottomless agony of the loss of a child. No words, especially the dry vocabulary of official reports, can capture what suffering is. It is a long way between New York and Baghdad. Whenever information made the journey, something was lost en route. It would have taken a huge leap of imagination sitting in a stuffy room on the banks of the East River to think about the real needs of Iraqi people: not in dollars and tons, but in human, emotional terms. Occasionally I tried, but it was too uncomfortable and unpleasant. I could not, for example, bring myself to watch John Pilger's film until long after I left the job. I didn't want to know what was happening there: it was easier to dismiss Pilger as a polemicist and carry on with our own version of reality.

One thing about this debate is now clear to me. We chose the "facts" to suit the policy, and not the other way around. Had we

been confronted with the unarguable truth of actual experience, we would not have found it so easy to do this. It was not only the junior diplomats in New York who were busy creating our own versions of what was "really" happening, it was the entire government. While we were arguing in New York, London would encourage us on. Together we would read the same reports from the UN in order to find in them even more egregious examples of Iraqi malfeasance, the more easily to argue our case that it was "all the Iraqi government's fault". Indeed there was plenty of such evidence. I clearly remember, dismal though the memory is, skim-reading dense and poorly-written UN reports, looking for the key sentences ("There has yet to be sufficient cooperation from the Iraqi government in implementing this aspect of the programme") to highlight in our telegrams back to London and then deploy like hand grenades in the negotiations. These sentences would stand out to me as if in bold type while the more nuanced information would fade almost literally into nothingness; and they became mini-factoids that would assume a life of their own, replayed first in our telegrams, then picked out by a desk officer in London for a ministerial press conference. If the minister remembered this factoid, he might use it in other interviews, and round and round it went.

This is not a problem that was unique to the arguments over Iraqi sanctions. It is common to all foreign policy and, despite the explosion of "information" in today's e-world, it seems to be getting worse. For the greater the amount of information, the greater the need for simplifying narratives to "explain" what is going on.

All information, however comprehensive it attempts to be, inevitably embodies a selection and reduction from reality. No one sees with the eyes of god. In the mass of available information,

inevitable selections have to be made about what to use in order to decide policy. In the British foreign service, there is an all-too-human tendency to seek out and relay the information that confirms our view of the world. And the further away one is from reality, the worse the tendency is. We were 6,000 miles from the Iraqi reality we were arbitrating; there were times when we might as well have been talking about the surface of the moon.

There is a belief in government that we, the policymakers, sit at the apex of a pyramid of information. No one in government is silly enough to believe that they know everything, but they have great faith that as the information about reality at the base of the pyramid is passed upward, only its unnecessary elements are filtered away, leaving only the essential "facts" for those at the summit on which to base their decisions. Civil service culture in Britain reifies the skill of taking large quantities of information and reducing it to the key essentials (the testing of this skill is a central part of the entrance examinations). From what I have seen of Germany and the US (two foreign services which I know better than others), other government services value this skill too. And it is easy to see why. The world is a complicated place. There is far too much information about everything. Decision-makers cannot possibly absorb all the information available, so they rely on reductions performed by those lower down the pyramid. But, as this episode illustrates, sometimes at least, what is essential may not be what is presented to the decision-maker; and indeed it may be the very thing that is left out. What was essential about decisions about sanctions on Iraq? I would argue that at least part of what was essential was the condition of the Iraqi people: their reality. And that reality played very little part in our deliberations. We talked about it; we even claimed to

care about it (remember the phrase which must have tripped across ministerial tongues a thousand times, "We have no quarrel with the Iraqi people"?). We thought we were talking about facts, or at least representations of facts, but they were the wrong ones.

Although we were wrong, we were confident in our wrongness. There were many others telling us we were wrong, but we ignored them. UN staff members, NGOs, ordinary Iraqis (including those who opposed Saddam) would tell us that sanctions were causing considerable suffering. But our assigned roles as diplomats gave us the confidence, some would say arrogance, to dismiss their concerns. They were suspect, politicised, motivated by sentiment or politics, whereas our motives rested on the elevated plane of diplomacy; if these motives were not pure, they were nonetheless the right ones for this discourse: we had "our" security, the region's security, even the world's security at heart.

Our physical location made such insouciance easier. It was very difficult for lobbyists or activists to know who we were. If they managed to identify us, it was harder still for them to meet us. We could simply refuse, leaving demonstrators to yell on the streets outside, far below our offices many storeys in the air. Our negotiations took place in small rooms deep inside the UN complex, inaccessible to all except those delegations allowed to attend. The press and outsiders could not get near. Since 9/11 the fencing and the security checks around these bastions of diplomacy have only become thicker.

If dissenters ever did manage to meet us, we could easily dismiss their arguments. Even if misguided, we were highly versed in the facts and nuances of the sanctions debate. Steeped in the reports, arguments and counter-arguments, we could easily outmanoeuvre

the earnest campaigners who came to present an alternative view, one perhaps more closely aligned to "reality".

The lesson is clear. Like the world, policy is complicated. At all times, the suffering of others should be given due heed, even priority above all other requirements. Policy-making does not benefit from secrecy or privacy. Karl Popper told us this many decades ago, but we have not yet learned his lesson. Information is not reliable, unless it is constantly re-examined, checked and tested against reality. Others, particularly those most affected by policy, must be allowed to participate, or at least to be heard.

4

WAR STORIES

WMD and Noble Half-Truths

Years after the United States and Britain invaded Iraq, the world remains polarised over the war. Supporters thought it necessary, while many opponents believe a false case was deliberately manufactured for it.[1]

This allegation has been reinforced by the discovery of a putative intellectual justification for such deceit, the idea of the "noble lie" propagated by the late University of Chicago philosopher Leo Strauss, one of the strongest intellectual influences on the neo-conservatives. According to Strauss, élites in liberal societies must sometimes create "myths" to hold those societies together, for fear that they would otherwise collapse through selfishness and individualism.

One such myth is the enemy, the threat, the identification and combating of which forces society to cohere and unite. Once that enemy was the Soviet Union and communism; today it is Al-Qaeda and Saddam Hussein's weapons of mass destruction.

This is a big allegation and it is a toxic dispute, poisonous to both domestic and international reputations, the cause of both angry ac-

cusation and equally bitter rebuttal. But perhaps the story of sanctions policymaking in the Security Council can help throw light on the argument.

While the two "sides" in the Security Council composed incompatible narratives of what was going on with sanctions against Iraq, both comprised and reinforced by partial selections of facts, something similar was going on in the story of Iraq and its weapons of mass destruction. This neither confirms nor fully refutes the "noble lie" thesis of deliberate deceit. It suggests, rather, a more complex and subtle, and if anything more disturbing, story.

Here the basis of evidence was not the UN, NGO or other reports on sanctions or sanctions-busting, many of which suffered their own peculiar biases and flaws, but a resource that is unavoidably unreliable, namely secret intelligence. Particularly after inspectors were withdrawn in late 1998, the available intelligence on Iraq was severely limited. Whatever Saddam had or did, he concealed under roofs or underground, and there is no aircraft or satellite camera yet invented that can penetrate there.

Both the United States and Britain were thus forced to rely on that most unreliable reporter of facts — human beings (or "humint" as it is known). In addition, there was the expert knowledge of the many inspectors who had visited Iraq's WMD sites and spoken with Iraqi officials and scientists. Despite these difficulties, the picture that emerged in the late 1990s and into 2002 was reasonably consistent.

This was that Iraq was not rearming to any great extent, that there were still questions about its disposal of past stocks of weapons, but in summary that the policy of containment was working. Inevitably, there were unanswered questions — unconfirmed reports of attempted imports of dual-use materials that might be used

to produce WMD and possibilities that the unaccounted-for dozen or so Scud missiles might still exist and be reassembled (not one was found postwar). But there was nothing that would suggest significant rearmament or intent to attack Iraq's neighbours, let alone Britain. The Butler Report[2] gives a similar account.

Yet, by September 2002, both the US and UK governments were claiming that Iraq was a significant threat, citing clear and authoritative intelligence evidence of rearmament and attempts to acquire nuclear, biological and chemical weapons. The US government went further, suggesting that Saddam Hussein, Al-Qaeda and 9/11 were somehow connected. Bush began to juxtapose Al-Qaeda and Saddam Hussein in adjacent sentences, never quite claiming a proven connection, but deliberately implying some kind of link. The implication, still repeated to this day by members of the Bush administration, was refuted by the 9/11 Commission. Even at the time of the war, Britain's Secret Intelligence Service (SIS) let it be known publicly that this suggestion had no foundation.

In *The Structure of Scientific Revolutions*, Thomas Kuhn cites a number of studies where scientists with different paradigmatic views observe different patterns in the same data — what he calls a switch in the visual *Gestalt*. For example, looking at a contour map, a student sees lines on a paper, a cartographer a picture of terrain. Only once trained will the student see the same as the cartographer, even though the data he is observing have not changed.

Both the British Prime Minister, to the Butler Review, and the former US Defense Secretary Donald Rumsfeld have admitted publicly (long after the war) that what changed before the war was not the evidence of Iraqi weapons but, in the new post-9/11 light, the appraisal of that evidence. The Prime Minister told the Butler

Review: "after September 11th it took on a completely different aspect…what changed for me with September 11th was that I thought then you have to change your mindset…you have to go out and get after the different aspects of this threat…you have to deal with this because otherwise the threat will grow…".

This rings true and is understandable. An event of the horror and magnitude of 9/11 should have changed our appreciation of the dangers of WMD and non-compliance with international law. It represented, for good or ill, a paradigm shift in the way our leaders saw the world. But it appears that not only did the appraisal change but so, crucially, did the presentation of that appraisal, and the evidence justifying it to the public.

No doubt other factors were at play. There is a tendency in government to see intelligence material as being at the pinnacle of the hierarchy of information. Unlike the voluminous flow of diplomatic telegrams, memos and open-source information that hits computers on desks across government every day, intelligence arrives in slim folders, adorned with colourful stickers announcing not only the secrecy of the information therein but the restricted circulation it enjoys. The impression thus given, a product of these aesthetics, is of access to the real thing, the secret core denied to all but the elite few.

History gives an interesting example of this phenomenon, namely the case of the Zinoviev letter. In 1924 Britain's Foreign Office was sent a copy of a letter, purporting to come from Grigori Zinoviev, the president of the Soviet Comintern, addressed to the central committee of the Communist Party of Great Britain. The letter urged the party to stir up the British proletariat in preparation for class war. The letter then appeared in the press, causing immense political and diplomatic repercussions. It was a major embarrassment for

the Prime Minister, Ramsay MacDonald, and the governing Labour Party. The opposition Conservatives won the general election four days later. Relations between Britain and the Soviet Union soured, and Anglo-Soviet treaties were abandoned.

Only in 1999, when the then Foreign Secretary Robin Cook ordered an investigation of Britain's official archives, was it confirmed that the Zinoviev letter was a fake. The fake was believed as genuine by the Foreign Office, the archives revealed, because it came from the Secret Intelligence Service (this an observation from the Foreign Office's own archival investigation).

An additional factor in Iraq was also that many of the human sources of intelligence had an understandable interest in exaggerating what they were reporting, not least because they wanted to encourage the overthrow of a regime they hated. The role of the Iraqi National Congress, the key Iraqi opposition group before the war, in providing "humint" is now well-known. But, interestingly, the Butler Review discounts this factor, pointing instead to the SIS's failure to validate its sources properly, the long reporting chains and the sources' lack of expertise on what they were reporting.

Back in the capitals, there is meanwhile an invisible undertow at work on the civil servants who collate and analyse this information. If ministers want a particular story to emerge, it has a way of emerging: the facts are made to fit the policy. It takes a brave if not foolhardy civil servant to resist this tide. This is not to claim that there was some secret cubicle in Whitehall (or Washington) where evidence of Iraq's weapons was deliberately fabricated, but something more subtle: evidence is selected from the available mass, contradictions are excised, and the selected data are repeated, rephrased, polished (and spun, if you prefer), until it seems neat,

coherent and convincing, to the extent that those presenting it may believe it fully themselves.

All of these reasons will have contributed to a considerable bias in the information that the government received and the analyses then produced on Iraq's WMD. All of these reasons should have inspired caution; any assessment based on such information should have been heavily caveated. But, as the Butler Report relates, instead of transmitting these caveats in its public presentations, such as the infamous Number 10 dossier, the government left them out. What was broadcast to the public was in effect not the summit of a hierarchy of information but a selection from a spectrum of information, a spectrum that ranged from the well-established to the highly speculative, and the selection came from the wrong end. Just as I once produced one-sided arguments to justify sanctions by ignoring all contrary evidence, the government produced a highly one-sided account of inherently unreliable information.

Of course governments in all democracies put forward one-sided accounts of policy. Economic statistics are always presented with the positive numbers in the forefront, the negative sidelined to footnotes or ignored. Civil servants are highly skilled in slanting information in this way. But there should be limits. When seeking to justify military action, the government has a duty to tell the whole truth, not just a partial account of it.

Something else was going on too. As the drums of war beat louder in Washington, both the US and UK governments became more strident in dismissing containment or other alternatives to all-out invasion. Bush declared sanctions to be as full of holes as a Swiss cheese; the Prime Minister, Tony Blair, even once, bizarrely, argued that military action was preferable to the distress caused by

sanctions. Sanctions were crumbling, the public was told (as it still is today). These governments gave the impression that all alternatives had been exhausted; war was the only option.

This was not in fact the case. There was a viable alternative. Effective action to seize Saddam Hussein's illegal financial assets and block oil smuggling would have denied him the resources which sustained his power: sanctions on the regime, and not its long-suffering people. For many years before the war this alternative was unfortunately never pursued with the necessary energy or commitment. The reasons for this are not immediately obvious.

Such a policy would have required consistent pressure across the region, applied to all of Iraq's neighbours. And, for different reasons in each case, it wasn't pursued with sufficient vigour. Senior envoys and ministers only rarely or half-heartedly mentioned smuggling in bilateral contacts, thereby implying toleration. Gradually it came to be understood that certain of Iraq's neighbours were "allowed" to import illegal oil, undermining attempts to deal with even the most egregious sanctions-busters.

Meanwhile, back in the Security Council, any attempt we made to propose collective action against smuggling was invariably blocked by France or Russia, on the alleged grounds that there was insufficient proof of the smuggling, or that such action might further harm Iraq's people. I lost count of the number of times we inserted provisions for sanctions-monitoring units, or other exhortations for action, into draft Council resolutions, only to have diplomats from these countries strike them out in negotiation (as veto-wielding permanent members, their acquiescence was essential for every dot and comma). The US and UK governments now like to claim that this was the reason sanctions failed (when in doubt, blame the

French); some even claim that the UN itself connived at corruption to benefit Saddam Hussein (an allegation for which there is scant evidence).[3] But, in truth, we too exerted precious little energy to enforce controls. While in New York we argued ourselves hoarse in negotiation, Washington and London rarely lifted a finger to pressure Iraq's neighbours to stem the illegal flows.

An effective anti-smuggling policy would have required an overarching and long-term strategy, addressing problems in a variety of different areas ranging from illegal bank accounts to cross-border oil smuggling. Such a strategy was never implemented. Instead there were piecemeal and ineffective efforts.

I suspect that the reason for this perhaps lies in the universal human truth that what can be left until later usually is, until it is too late. The policy was difficult, complex and unfashionable, demanding extensive study to master and discuss, a luxury that busy ministers and senior officials do not enjoy. It was never the first or most glamorous priority, so it was allowed to slide.

In the end, when contrasted with the complexity and uncertainty of the alternatives, war may have seemed simpler. In the strange way that governments are swept along by events without properly stopping to think, war came to be seen as the only viable course, a current no doubt strengthened in Britain by the clear determination in Washington, now amply chronicled (in Bob Woodward's *Plan of Attack*, among others), to pursue conflict.

It would undoubtedly have taken considerable political and diplomatic effort to corral Iraq's neighbours and other states into this alternate course. It would not have had the binary clarity of winning or losing a war. But this effort would certainly have been less than that of going to war, and it had the real potential to remove

the regime by cutting away the funds that sustained it. Above all, this approach would not have incurred the sacrifice of Iraqi, British, American and other lives.

If Iraq was not a threat and not collaborating with terrorists, why did the Bush and Blair governments go to war with it? Several plausible explanations have been offered by others: the US administration's need after 9/11 to demonstrate its power — anywhere, anyhow; a *mission civilisatrice* to democratise the world by force, an impulse given strength by the vigorous and forceful lobby of the Iraqi opposition. But less credible, given the record on sanctions, is the claim that the welfare of the Iraqi people was the primary concern.

Another possible explanation lies in the more sinister motives of oil and its control. The prospect of Iraq's huge reserves (the second largest in the world) hung in the air throughout the policy deliberations in the years before the war. It was well-known that Saddam Hussein had allocated all the massively lucrative post-sanctions exploration contracts to French, Chinese, Russian and other non-US and non-British companies (and it bothered the companies a lot, as they would tell us). It is hard to believe that the immense potential for money-making and energy security did not exert some pull in the decision to invade, but the evidence for some sort of conspiracy led by Big Oil is hard to come by. But again, we do not know, because we have not been told. Instead we were given not the "noble lie", but the somewhat less-than-noble half-truth. The full answer will perhaps be revealed by the chief protagonists in years to come. For now, all we can know for sure is that the empirical reasons these governments have given so far simply do not add up.

Perhaps, therefore, a non-empirical reason is at the heart of this. They did it because they thought it was right. Saddam Hussein was

a bad man, a potential danger in the future, not today. And this, if true, is a legitimate reason, or at least arguable. Unfortunately, it is neither the primary reason both governments gave the UN or their peoples for going to war (though both President Bush and Prime Minister Blair allude to it with ever greater frequency), nor is it justifiable in any canon of international law (although perhaps it should be).

And here we return to Leo Strauss: not to the "noble lie", but to his belief in "natural law", a fundamental, sometimes religious (though Strauss, I read, was an atheist) sense of right and wrong, a right and wrong superior to all other laws — including, it seems in this case, international law. Both leaders have said in the past that they believe in such rules, as I suspect most of us do in some way. And it is perhaps the readiness of voters, especially in the US, to accept this reasoning that lies behind the curious phenomenon that, although the evidence that these governments misled their peoples was soon clear, neither Bush nor Blair paid any immediate political price for it.

In the 2004 presidential elections the allegation of lying, noble or otherwise, and the decidedly ambiguous course of the resulting war did not turn the people against their chosen president. His "natural law" argument — that it was right to remove the Iraqi dictator — sufficed, even when the empirical evidence did not. Tony Blair likewise was comfortably re-elected in Britain in 2005.

Political theorists of the twenty-first century have much to feed on in this analysis: it is a story rich in paradox and contradiction, from which it is hard to divine rational inferences or laws. The governments did not manufacture lies, but neither did they tell the truth, even when they thought they did. These half-truths, moreo-

ver, bore no relation whatever to the real truth of what was actually
going on in Iraq (no terrorists, no WMD). And in the end, the elec-
tors, in the name of whose security and safety the whole exercise
was undertaken, do not seem to care much either way. In this picture it seems that neither Strauss nor Plato (who in fact originated
the "noble lie") nor anyone else is much of a guide. Things seem
altogether less ordered and coherent than any logical analysis would
have it. The key actors claim to have agency, to make rational decisions, but in fact are swept along by forces they cannot grasp. Laws
of democracy and morality give way: the law of chaos instead must
hold sway.

Here may be the biggest misperception of all, though not a lie,
since it is hardly conscious. This is a misperception — a fiction, if
you like — in which governments and governed collaborate, for
to believe otherwise is too uncomfortable. And this is that governments, politicians and civil servants are able to observe the world
without bias and disinterestedly interpret its myriad signs into facts
and judgments (indeed, in the Foreign Office, telegrams are divided
into these two very categories: "Detail" and "Comment") with an
objective, almost scientific rigour. The story of what these two governments observed, believed and then told their populations about
Iraq suggests an altogether more imperfect reality.

5

THEM AND US

Essentialism and the Cult of "We"

"Nations! What are nations? Tartars, and Huns, and Chinamen! Like insects, they swarm. The historian strives in vain to make them memorable. It is for want of a man that there are so many men. It is individuals that populate the world."

Henry David Thoreau, Life Without Principle

Diplomacy is often compared to games like chess. Indeed, chess pieces frequently adorn the covers of books or websites about diplomacy. Diplomacy is depicted as an intricate sport where victory is the object, and the movements, motives and capabilities of the teams are finite and knowable, even if they can be complex.[1]

In order to play chess, you need two sides, clearly delineated: one white, one black. So it is to play diplomacy. In order for diplomacy to function as a discourse, to make any sense, and to perpetuate itself in its current form, the sides involved are required to delineate themselves into discrete sets: Us and Them.

Essentialising Us

When a diplomat speaks to the microphone outside the UN Security Council or is interviewed on CNN, invariably he or she will talk about "we". Secretary of State Condoleezza Rice does it, the State Department press spokesman does it. Individual diplomats do it.

"We seek the disarmament of Iran and are dissatisfied with their assurances to date."

"We welcome the recent elections in Ukraine."

"Our interests in China versus those in Taiwan dictate the continuation of the One-China policy."

This was how I spoke with journalists. It was how I talked in negotiations with other diplomats: "We do not agree with your proposed text for paragraph 12 of the resolution and instead offer the following words…". Even in our internal meetings, we spoke in this way: "This morning our objective in the Security Council discussion should be to…". Our internal telegrams discussing policy discussed what "we" should do about country x or y.

This manner of speaking is a reflection of the way the world is. International relations is seen, and practised, very much as a business of states interacting with one another, with diplomats the formal exponents of that process, authorised to speak in the name of their state. Chinese diplomats will speak of China's wishes as those of a single entity, despite the massive size and diversity of that country. It is an expression of the reality that the state remains, for good or ill, the organising unit of contemporary international affairs.

It may therefore seem naïve — even quixotic — to question whether such a system is the right one. But delving into the process

by which a group of people are assigned the right to determine (or even invent) the wishes of the state reveals some troubling insights. In order for the diplomat to articulate his country's wishes, those wishes must be boiled down into a discrete set of desiderata. This process inevitably involves simplification but, as we see in the next chapter, it is an arbitrary process and one resting on some questionable assumptions of what foreign policy is "about". The creation of a separate political and moral identity for a group of people — the policymakers of foreign policy — must inevitably risk artifice, arbitrariness and, as I have argued elsewhere, a lack of accountability.

If the diplomatic "we" is arbitrating what the state wants (and thus how the world is run), how is this identity developed and maintained, and what values does it embody? In short, who is "we"?

Before I joined the British diplomatic service, I gave little thought to what it was to be British. I was just me. But by some subterranean and unexplained process when you join the Foreign Office, you begin to identify yourself with the state. In both speech, writing, and — more insidiously — thought, I became "we". A singular became a plural. How did this transformation take place?

When I entered the Foreign Office in 1989, all new entrants were required to undergo what was called "induction training". Our group of about a dozen eager twenty-somethings was sent to an otherwise anonymous building off Millbank, near to the Houses of Parliament. Almost as soon as my fellow new entrants and I were sitting in a large grey room where our training took place, our instructor began to talk to us, and he talked about "we".

"I'm here to tell you about the way we do things in the Foreign Office", he said. We then learned about the correct way to address ministers, the correct way to compose a minute (not a memo, but a

minute), a telegram and a submission. We learned that minutes (not memos) to under-secretaries and above, including ministers, were to be written on "blue" paper, or simply just "blue". The only twist to this otherwise straightforward procedure was that "blue" paper was in fact green, a lovely twilled paper, rich and textured. Very expensive, it looked, and very green. We were not told why blue was green. My fellow new entrants and I were charmed by these quaint traditions.

But nor were we told who "we" were. It was simply assumed that "we" in the Foreign Office were Britain. This assumption suffused everything we were taught and subsequently did in our Foreign Office careers. It began at the beginning and quickly became a habit of speech and writing. It became a habit of thought: I became "we". Even after I had resigned from the Foreign Office, I found myself saying "we think that the Zimbabwean government needs to…". "We" was wired deep.

A feisty young diplomat from the British mission in Pretoria gave us a lecture about how "we" thought sanctions on apartheid South Africa were a bad idea (these were the days of Margaret Thatcher's policy of "constructive engagement"). A diplomatic dispatch was presented to us as an example of how to write such pieces. In it, the ambassador wrote about how "we" had got this country "wrong" and "we" needed a new approach. In a number of different ways, we were taught how "we" saw the world. What we were never taught, however, was *how* it was that "we" saw the world that way. That "we" saw it that way and that "we" were the arbiters of what Britain wanted was taken for granted.

Part of our training was a game. The Foreign Office invented a policy exercise about a crisis in a fictional country called Boremeya

and what "we" should do about it. It was a good game, and fun. It
lasted about a day and consisted of crisis meetings, submissions to
ministers ("make sure to use the blue paper!") and difficult encoun-
ters with the Boremeyan Foreign Minister, played by one of our
instructors. Throughout the game, the new entrants were told to
consider what "we" wanted or needed in the situation. At several
points, what we wanted was put into other terms: what are our
"interests" in this situation? A British company was negotiating a
contract with the Boremeyan government when a political crisis
erupted, forcing us to reappraise the situation and advise the minister on what "our" policy should be.

The foreign services of other countries give more extended
training to their neophyte diplomats before letting them loose on
the world. The German foreign ministry, at the more intensive
end of the spectrum, requires its new entrants to spend two taxing
years at the Auswärtiges Amt's training school, where they are
taught a great deal of history, diplomatic practice, rules of protocol and, above all, law. Fully-qualified lawyers who join the German diplomatic service, and there are many of them, are excused
the second year of training. In other words, all German diplomats
have a minimum of one year's fulltime training in international
law. We had none. If we wanted to learn about international law
we could, if we wished (it was entirely voluntary) attend a two-
week course at Cambridge University.

This thin education in law however did not prevent us from being
told, with frequent repetition, that Britain stood for the "rule of
law" or a "world of rules". This was one of the core characteristics which British diplomacy claimed to represent. Never was this
statement of belief analysed; it was presented to us as a given and

one furthermore that we should ourselves propagate henceforward. Although we were not taught "the rule of law", we were taught that British diplomats stood for it.

It was a similar story with economics. German diplomats-in-training spent months learning economics. In the Foreign Office, those without economics training were not encouraged to get any but, if they were so disposed, they could attend another two-week training course which, it was alleged, took the trainee to "degree level". Again, this did not prevent the repeated assertion of the belief that "Britain" and therefore "we" believed in market economics and the promotion of trade as core values.

Beyond the thought-habit of thinking as "we", there is another way that new diplomats are inculcated into identifying themselves with the state. In the case of the British Foreign Office, it begins before you even join, when you must undergo a process known as "positive vetting". There is a similar process in the US and other major foreign services.

After I had passed the many entrance exams and interviews to get into the diplomatic service, the Security Department of the Foreign Office assigned an investigator (in my case, a former policeman) to examine my background, and quiz my acquaintances and friends, in order to ensure that I would not pose a security risk to the government. Without this clearance I could not begin work since much that the Foreign Office does involves access to "Top Secret" material, the compromise of which, in theory at least, poses a grave risk to the security of the state. Others who had gone before told me that the process was straightforward "as long as you don't tell them anything". Unfortunately for me, my personal referees had already told my investigator various things, including the fact that

I occasionally drank too much at university and that I was sharing a flat with a gay man. I took the naïve view that since I had nothing in my life to be ashamed of, I would tell them the truth. This approach proved to be a mistake.

My vetting took place as the Cold War was ending, in 1989. But the Foreign Office still feared the pernicious attentions of the KGB and others, and it was felt that being homosexual risked exposing the officer to blackmail. It did not seem to have occurred to the mandarins in charge of the Security Department that a blanket prohibition on homosexuality was more likely to force serving or potential Foreign Office officers to lie about their true sexual natures and thus increase their vulnerability to blackmail.[2] So my vetting officer subjected me to a long series of absurd and insulting questions about my sexuality, culminating in the conclusive, "So you've never been tempted off the straight and narrow then?". To which I could honestly answer, "No".

Meanwhile, my vetting officer had found out from my application forms that my grandmother was Polish. Poland was at that time undergoing its transition to democracy. But the inquisitor felt, following policy, that the mere fact that I had Polish relations posed a security risk, since the KGB might "get at" them and use them to "get at" me (it had happened in the past when Poland was a vassal of the Soviet Union). My family was thus forced to dig up long-buried family records and inform the Foreign Office exactly when, where and how all my Polish ancestors had died (in order that the KGB couldn't discover their names and impersonate them to "target" me). In the process, they made the upsetting discovery that some of them, as members of the Polish resistance, had died in Auschwitz.

I was obliged to attend several interviews with the investigator in a sparse office in another anonymous building near Parliament Square, furnished with sinister-looking steel filing cabinets. His desk, like that of a *film noir* interrogator, had no papers and just one government-issue swivel lamp, the only light in the otherwise gloomy room. The interviews would sometimes last for hours. I wouldn't be told how long. My family and friends were at first amused by his questions, but soon became irritated and in some cases deeply upset (my flatmate was — understandably — especially offended).

My first entry date into the Foreign Office came and went, and I had not passed my "PV" as positive vetting is known. My personnel officer seemed to take pleasure in telling me that it was extremely unlikely that I would eventually be allowed in. I swallowed these humiliations — I wanted too badly to become a member of that rarefied species, a diplomat. Meanwhile, I was forced to find temporary work for a further few months until the next entry date came up when, against expectations, the now-completed investigations had convinced The Office, as my investigator called it (and as I too would come to know it), that I was not gay, communist, a drunk, a drug addict or a debtor, and I was at last invited to attend my first day of work.

The inculcation does not stop there. When you join the Foreign Office, and once you have been "positively vetted", you are required to sign the Official Secrets Act. This draconian document comprises your agreement never in your lifetime to reveal to outsiders or to publicise in any way the content of your work. With astonishing breadth, the act defines the information that you must protect to your grave as any official business, determined by the government itself. In other words, anything that you do in the course of your

work is to be kept secret, forever. Any revelation about what that work entailed (such as this book for instance) is in theory a criminal offence. When I was offered the document to sign (it was mailed to me at home), I did not hesitate. The glamour of secrecy lured me in, and I simply never believed that the day might come when its strictures might seem more a threat than an invitation.

The signature of the Official Secrets Act marks one initiation into the culture of secrecy that pervades government, and particularly those parts of it dealing with foreign policy. When you learn how to handle documents, for instance, you are taught that the originator of the document must classify it, using designations starting with "restricted" up to "top secret". You are taught that only those documents that would not perturb you if they were handed out to passers-by on the street can be designated "unclassified". Unsurprisingly therefore, almost every document produced inside the Foreign Office is classified "restricted" or above.

This culture is constantly reinforced throughout one's career. Telegrams are transmitted only when highly encrypted. All computers are hardened against electronic eavesdropping. Telephones carry stickers warning against divulging state confidences. So many and so ubiquitous are these limitations that it is soon clear that the only people one can discuss candidly what "we" are doing are one's colleagues — other members of the club of "we". For what "we" are doing is the affairs of state, and other states might try to find out our secrets; therefore one should only talk to people with a "need to know". This excludes almost everyone, including those in whose name "we" are acting.

The creation of the identity of a British diplomat, the exponent of the state, can seem a process which is innocent, unloaded and

necessary. It could be argued that such a process is requisite for the international system the world today enjoys. States interact in this system; therefore the system requires exponents of the state's wishes, steeped in the richest sense of what their nation stands for. But my experience suggests that intrinsic in this process of diplomatic identity-creation is something dangerous.

In spite of the almost complete absence of outside scrutiny, the British Foreign Office does not "do" self-criticism. Embedded within the acculturation process is a deep sense that "we" are in the right. From the day I stepped into the training department, to the day I left my last full job at the UK Mission in New York, it was part of the air I breathed that what "we" were offering the world was good. The world's oldest parliamentary democracy, a successful economy, an ancient culture, we represented the acme of what the rest of the world should aspire to. We were moreover pragmatic and "sensible" (never idealist, that was too romantic and therefore silly). American diplomacy, though marked with different emphases (the infinitely variable notion of "freedom"),[3] is little different. Even when our motives were transparently different, we were encouraged, subtly and through imitation, to claim that we were offering others versions of ourselves: our democracy, our laws, our "values". In Afghanistan in 2002, our policy was framed as the delivery of stability and democracy, even when our motive was solely (and not illegitimately) our own security. I believed this identity: it made me feel better (particularly when defending the effects of sanctions in Iraq) and it gave me purpose. I only stopped believing it when the contrary evidence became too compelling to ignore. And even then the abandonment of this persona was a painful and drawn-out business.

This self-regard breeds a pervasive complacency. If our motives are always pure, it follows that "we" cannot be wrong. When Britain failed to secure the infamous "second" resolution authorising an invasion of Iraq, officials were very quick to blame France (for threatening a veto), rather than acknowledging the reality of "our" failure to garner sufficient support.[4] Examination of Britain's failure (with others) to stop the genocide in Bosnia was left to journalists and scholars:[5] no comprehensive internal inquiry was instigated. These are but two of the more blatant examples of a culture that brooks no self-examination while resisting meanwhile the rigour of external scrutiny.

British diplomats are not alone in maintaining a comfortable and flattering self-image. In my experience, diplomats of many other countries rest on similar conceits. An Egyptian might claim that his tradition is one of brokering the pan-Arab view (a Nasserist inheritance) while offering a bridge between East and West (a role claimed too by Turkish diplomats); the Dutch are the hard-headed pragmatists of the European Union; the Singaporeans are the politically-incorrect realists, and so on. No one is the bad guy. Everyone believes they are serving the Good. There is a degree of caricature here, but in that caricature lies an uncomfortable truth: that to a greater or lesser degree, diplomats are required to define themselves, to create an identity, in order to function.

Essentialising Them

Thus is one side of the chess board delineated: "Us". But for the game to be played, the other team needs to be defined, or essen-

tialised, too: "Them". Without such delineation, the game cannot be played.[6]

Diplomacy requires a system of ordering to function; thought requires such a system too (or so some philosophers would argue). In diplomacy it is not seen as a mistake to boil the world down to some simple essence; it is mandatory. The easiest way to pretend that you understand the world is to essentialise it. The Arabs (all of them) are this; the Israelis are that. The Thais are a little bit…the Malaysians far too…and the French, well, the French are always incredibly… .

You will see this kind of essentialism practised every day. You need only open your newspaper. There you will read how the US President describes the aspirations of the Iranian people for freedom and democracy (though curiously in 2006 he no longer does so when talking about the Iraqi people, whose behaviour since their "liberation" has suggested that more complicated ambitions may also be at play). Switch on your television and analysts talk about the needs of the "people of the Middle East" or the approach "the Europeans" take to building democracy (often in the American discourse the appellation "the Europeans" carries negative overtones). And it is not only the West which indulges in such characterisations. In April 2006 Egypt's President Mubarak upset sensibilities across the Middle East by suggesting in an interview that Iraq's Shia, indeed all Shia in the Middle East, were more loyal to Iran than they were to their own countries.

Twenty years since Edward Said's *Orientalism*, his excoriating critique of western characterisations of the Middle East, diplomats still orientalise almost the whole world, reducing its complexities and uncertainties to simple cultural and racial stereotypes. Routinely,

you can still hear diplomats talking (and some journalists do it too) about *the Arab street*, a place where presumably Arabs gather to talk and express opinions (furtively, presumably). (In my *Economist* this week is a review of three books about "the Arabs", including one by an Arab, which in different ways analyse why the Arabs have difficulty assimilating democracy. The piece is titled "Not yet, say the Arabs".) Or you can hear China explained in terms of the way "they", the Chinese, think, all 1.2 billion of them.

I have been working for some time in Kosovo. When talking about this place, many western diplomats and foreign policy analysts talk about the need for Kosovo to "progress"; that its majority-Albanian culture is "clan-based", its values are those of "loyalty and revenge" rather than "our" more enlightened ways. As for their political ambitions, they just want a greater Albania. More than one senior UN official told me that "these people" were "primitive".

Having lived in Kosovo, it is hard to recognise these descriptions. No one I met talked about their "clan". Many Kosovars I know are among the most hospitable, friendly but also urbane people I've met. Many speak several languages (something many American and British diplomats do not). No one has ever mentioned in my hearing a desire to unify with Albania (a very different country from Kosovo). There are also Kosovars who do not share these attractive characteristics, but that is the point. Essentialism always leaves someone out.

The production of these depictions is sometimes trivial, but nonetheless revealing of the mindset. On my first ever overseas posting, to Norway, I wrote a letter — at the encouragement of my boss — to the Western European Department in London analysing the "Norwegian national character". This letter was superficial in the

extreme, mainly because its observations had been gathered from watching the behaviour of Norwegians at the luggage carousel at Oslo airport when I first arrived. I spoke no Norwegian (and never did). This did not however prevent me from sending the letter.

This kind of thing is, I hope, less common today than it was then (in the early 'nineties). But you will still find ambassadors and embassies routinely generalising about the cultures and "national characters" of the countries where they are hosted: they do it because, as I was, they are encouraged to. If you are sitting in an office in Whitehall, or Foggy Bottom, you want your embassies to explain the world to you, so that you can feel you understand it. You are part of a pyramid of reductionism and you cannot escape it. As an official, you are required to tell your minister or Secretary of State that you understand the world. If you are a minister or Secretary of State, you are obliged to say to your legislature, or the press, that you understand what is going on in, say, Iran or China. The Secretary of State cannot give a ten-week seminar on China's complexities; they have to be summed up in a few sentences (or less). In these analyses, you cannot admit to uncertainty or even complexity. Essentialism is, unfortunately, essential. The question however is whether such reductionism helps or hinders our struggle to understand the world.

As a diplomat, you are moreover abetted by your foreign colleagues in the discourse. Just as the British diplomat essentialises his own country into what "we" want, they will essentialise theirs. Without hesitation the German diplomat, in describing his views about the genocide in Rwanda, or democracy in Russia, will speak as Germany — "we think intervention is impracticable". The Egyptian will do the same, and the Russian likewise. Thus one can report their

views as "Germany's", "Egypt's" or "Russia's"; and in my telegrams from New York I would describe them in just this way, sometimes without even recording the real names of the individual diplomats I had spoken to, just their countries. Oddly, the only diplomats I have found who don't indulge in this manner of speaking are those new to the diplomatic scene: the Somalilanders and the Kosovars. They have yet to learn the habit of generalisation.

A recent scientific study analysed the characteristics of different nationalities, asking whether there was any truth to well-worn national stereotypes. Researchers for the National Institute on Aging (NIA) in the US examined the accuracy of national character stereotypes in forty-nine cultures worldwide. They asked nearly four thousand people to describe the "typical" member of their own culture.[7]

When researchers compared the average trait levels, i.e. the cultural group's true attributes to the stereotypes, there was no agreement. For example, Americans believe the typical American is very assertive, and Canadians believe the typical Canadian is submissive, but in fact Americans and Canadians have almost identical scores on measures of assertiveness. Looking at each other's personality traits, the researchers found that Indian citizens see themselves as unconventional and open to a wide range of new experiences, but measurements of personality show that they are more conventional than the rest of the people in the world. Czechs believe that they are antagonistic and disagreeable, but when personality is actually observed, they score higher than most people in the world on measures of altruism and modesty.

One of the study's leaders, Dr Robert McCrae, said "People should understand that we are all prone to these kinds of precon-

ceptions and likely to believe that they are justified by our experience, when in fact they are often unfounded stereotypes. We need to remind ourselves to see people as individuals, whether they are Americans or Lebanese, Gen Xers or senior citizens" (the NIA's objective was in part to disprove preconceptions about age groups, particularly older ones).

Diplomacy is still often ignorant of this lesson, preferring to talk of national characteristics, countries as single, uniform entities and, if they are not conveniently uniform (like the Japanese or the Dutch), of their subgroups and ethnicities. It would not surprise Said to discover that, in western diplomatic systems like Britain or the US, the tendency to essentialise other countries increases the more unlike us these countries are. In the annual ambassadorial dispatches and telegrams, the ambassador in Germany is much less likely to generalise about "the Germans" or the cultural identity of Germany than the ambassador reporting from Riyadh. In the American discourse, it is routine to generalise about "the Europeans". Hardly anyone in Europe, notably, even uses the term.

One curious manifestation of this way of thinking is what happens to language when national generalisations fail. Before the invasion of Iraq in 2003, British and American diplomats and politicians would routinely talk about the Iraqi people as a homogeneous whole, as in "sanctions are not intended to harm the Iraqi people", "we have no quarrel with the Iraqi people, just with the leadership", or, as the invasion approached, "the Iraqi people yearn for their liberation".

After the invasion, and as sectarian and religious tensions emerged into violent confrontation, the language changed. Commentators and leaders alike began to talk about the "Shi-ites", "the Baathists", "the Sunnis" and, just as they did formerly with the "Iraqi people",

they ascribed collective characteristics to these groups, as in "the Sunnis feel threatened by Shia dominance" or "the Kurds want their own state".

I once attended a lecture by a former British diplomat who found himself, post-invasion, governor of an entire province of Iraq. To explain the complexities of his environment, he began to draw circles on a board, inscribing within them the names of Iraq's different ethnic groups and then drawing lines and arrows to indicate the relationship between them. He clearly needed such a delineated system to help him understand what was going on. But to realise the deficiencies of any such system, one need only apply it to one's own reality: Britain's "middle classes want economic growth and social stability", "America's blacks support the Democrats". We feel insulted when others do it to us. Anti-Americanism is built on simplistic caricatures which grossly misdescribe America's massive diversity. As a Briton living in America, my hackles rise whenever I hear a sentence beginning, "the Brits are...". It is crass to describe our own societies in such terms, but this is what diplomats and analysts routinely to do other societies, and it is always inaccurate.

Diplomats don't think and talk like this because they are racist. Most are not, and love the wider world; they do so because it reduces the world's complexity to something that can be ordered and put into a system: made sense of.

Moreover this habit of essentialising is a practice that reflects the way the diplomatic world actually *is*. Diplomats speak of what China wants in a draft Security Council text because the Chinese ambassador says "China wants paragraph 12 deleted...". It is not only essentialising, it is also a reflection of diplomatic and political reality. But it is a self-reinforcing reality, and for that reinforcement

to function there must be a process of essentialising performed both upon ourselves (as I describe above) and upon them. In negotiations at the UN Security Council, I realised that part of the way in which we worked out what we — Britain — wanted was by distinguishing our wishes from those with whom we saw ourselves in natural competition (France or Russia). So subtle and insidious was this process that it is hard to offer convincing proof, except to say that more often than I would want to admit we saw issues such as sanctions on Iraq not primarily in terms of the issue itself but as a means of getting what "we" wanted (this "competitive" model of diplomacy is discussed further in chapter 6). And what "we" wanted was sometimes defined in terms of what they — our opponents — didn't want.

A paradoxical example of the boiling down of what we and they want is to be found in trade negotiations. International trade talks at the WTO — the most recent being the so-called "Doha Round" — often revolve around the trading of concessions between national delegations (or groups of delegations). One of the most common "concessions" is the granting of trade access to the domestic market of the state offering the concession. Such concessions are offered in exchange for access to others' markets in the same or different products, in a highly-complex bargaining process. The offering of such "concessions" is however bunkum, because the benefits of free trade flow more to the importer than the exporter: imports of cheaper or better goods give consumers more for their money and, through competition, raise domestic productivity.[8] In other words, what is being offered is not a concession at all — the party offering the concession is proposing something that will benefit it more. But so familiar have the discourse of trade talks and the calculus of con-

cession-based bargaining become that everyone pretends that what is not a concession is one, and vice versa.

It is no coincidence that it is governments that perform this essentialising. They must. It is profoundly in the interest of government, and the politicians who lead it, to claim that only they can speak for the whole country. Equally, therefore, they must affirm the nature of the international system by accepting that other governments speak for their whole countries. A modern diplomat would deny that they are so crass as to essentialise other cultures and countries in the way I have described. Of course, they aver, that when they talk about Iran's policy, they mean the policy of the Iranian government, and indeed that is often how they will describe it.

But the habit of referring to whole countries in the singular and to their government as the embodiment of that state is one as deep-rooted as the state-based international system itself. To change the nomenclature of the actors would be to remove the assumption that governments represent the totality or indeed the diversity of their countries. This would alter the nature of the international system from one based around states as the unit of agency to one based on some other unit or units. But as long as governments wish to hold sway in international policy and decision-making, they must continually reaffirm not only their own but each other's legitimacy to speak for their countries, even when the government is as undemocratic as, say, Muammar Gadhafi's in Libya.

Perhaps one reason why this habit persists is because of the way that diplomacy evolved. From its origins in Classical times, through the Middle Ages and the development of the state-based system of the Peace of Westphalia, diplomats represented — and negotiated between — discrete entities: cities, provinces and later states.

In contrast to today, the business between them was limited to relatively narrow areas like war and peace, and trade. These were important but they did not have the character of the massive and diverse contacts and interactions (words which do not by themselves adequately convey the complex and dynamic nature of these flows) of today's world.

One of the seminal texts that helped define the nature of diplomacy is *De la manière de négocier avec les souverains, de l'utilité des negotiations, du choix des ambassadeurs et des envoyez, et des qualitez necessaries pour réussir dans ces employs,* published by François de Callières in Paris in 1716. De Callières saw the principal function of diplomacy as moderating and managing the clash of conflicting interests as efficiently as possible. Thus it was important for diplomats to be honest in their dealings. Diplomatic immunity was also to be upheld, not merely because of legal provisions but because the interests of princes compelled it. The diplomatist would be the agent rather than the architect of policy, but would be crucial both in the framing of policy and even more in the business of seeking to persuade representatives of other governments to see matters in this rather than that light. He would be required to assess how the interests of his state and the other state could be met on terms acceptable to both.

From this summary one can see how remarkably similar this conception of diplomacy is to the way it is usually conceived today. Yet the world we live in today is remarkably different. The post-war establishment of new multilateral diplomatic machineries such as the United Nations, NATO and the European Union — while creating new forums for state-to-state interactions — has not altered the fundamental idea that diplomacy is about states identifying their interests and arbitrating them with one another. Indeed, these insti-

tutions are premised on the very notion that states can meet there and decide upon their common problems. It is therefore no surprise that diplomats tend to make the world and its myriad problems fall into these shapes. That this process is becoming more and more artificial and disconnected from the reality of the forces at work in the world is not yet evident enough to compel change.

Essentialising the World

It is far too disconcerting a prospect for governments or the diplomats who represent them to analyse or talk about the world as it really is, one shaped and affected by multitudinous and complex forces, among which governments are but one group of many involved. To preserve their own role, and the belief — comforting to us as well to them — that governments are "in charge" of events, they must continually assert that governments are on top of the pile of agents and must determine what is important and what is to be done, and make and enforce the rules.

This may have been appropriate in 1648 or 1945. But today the trouble is that the world is growing more and more complicated. Its problems are ever less susceptible to the essentialising analysis traditional in diplomacy. Everyone, including the diplomats, accepts that many of our most troubling problems are transnational in nature — pollution, bird flu, terrorism — complex in their causes and thus solutions, and require mass action to tackle. The division of the world into the coloured pieces of the board game makes less and less sense. It always was a simplification, but it is becoming an ever more absurd one.

Globalisation in some respects implies a greater simplicity, for instance the narrowing of the world into one market. But even those who believe this must also acknowledge the world's continuing if not burgeoning complexity. Was it conceivable thirty years ago that the fury of one young Egyptian over the war in Chechnya would lead him to fly an aircraft into the World Trade Centre in New York, an act facilitated by an organisation born of Osama bin Laden's anger against the US occupation of Saudi Arabia, and itself given a base by a fundamentalist regime in Afghanistan, whose assumption of control was a direct consequence of Soviet occupation and slow decline (and this itself is a simplified account of a complex series of causes and events)? This singular act, itself the progenitor of massive, complex and unforeseeable change, was brilliantly anatomised in the 9/11 Commission Report, which took nearly 400 pages to describe the antecedents and chronology of this single event.

The reductionist tendency in diplomacy is reinforced by, and itself reinforces, the commentary we read in the press. Oddly, the more complicated our globalising world becomes, the more those commenting on it tend to such simplification. Confounded by the world's complexity, we grope for simplifying metaphors — the big idea — to explain what is going on. Academics and commentators duly oblige, offering up "the world is flat", "the clash of civilisations" or "the moment" (when America could save the world).

Those consuming these nostrums have perhaps only themselves to blame. The outlets of the mass media are in sharp competition. The measured commentary attracts less attention than the sensational. A recent study by Philip E. Tetlock[9] confirms the suspicion: those offering the most dramatic political predictions attract the most press attention, but are unsurprisingly the most inaccurate.

His study examined predictions from thousands of experts about the fates of dozens of countries, and then scored the predictions for accuracy. His team found that the media not only failed to weed out bad ideas, but often favoured them, especially when the truth was too messy to be packaged neatly.

Tetlock's evidence falls into two categories: optimists and pessimists (or "boomsters" and "doomsters", as he calls them). Between 1985 and 2005, boomsters made ten year forecasts that exaggerated the chances of big positive changes in both financial markets (e.g. a Dow Jones Industrial Average of 36,000) and world politics (e.g. tranquillity in the Middle East and dynamic growth in sub-Saharan Africa). They assigned probabilities of 65% to rosy scenarios that materialised only 15% of the time.

In the same period doomsters performed even more poorly, exaggerating the chances of negative changes in all the same places where boomsters accentuated the positive, plus several more (including the prediction of the disintegration of Canada, Nigeria, India, Indonesia, South Africa, Belgium, and Sudan). They assigned probabilities of 70% to bleak scenarios that materialized only 12% of the time. But despite these gross inaccuracies, these "over-claimers" rarely paid any penalties for being wrong. On the contrary, the media showered lavish attention on them while neglecting their more careful (and accurate) colleagues.

There is perhaps something unstated at play here. Our attachment to simple models of the world and grand overstatement may be related to the diplomat's need — which I could once identify as my own — to attribute to themselves a beneficent rather than a malign persona. We need narratives of ourselves and of the world to explain it. And we are unlikely to choose negative ones (if not

for others, at least for ourselves). Just as we need to view ourselves in a positive light, we desperately want the world to make sense, to respond to order and systematisation. It is paradoxical that within this innocent-seeming desire lies acute danger.

As we shall see in the next chapters, these biases in the way the world is described to us, and is arbitrated by policymakers, contribute to error. Indeed, they may compound one another and thus compound the failure. A complex system (is it even a system?) is described and governed by those who prefer to see it in simpler terms than it actually is. Unfortunately for its would-be players (and for those who would comment on them), the world is not a chessboard.

6

THE TELEGRAM OR HOW TO BE IGNORED

UN Security Council and Tindouf, Algeria

One of the principal artefacts of diplomatic business is the encrypted telegram between the embassy and the capital. In the British Foreign Office, telegram writing is a highly fetishised business. The drafting process is stylised and hierarchical, in a way an unconscious metaphor for the whole business of diplomacy.

If a junior diplomat writes the first draft, it must be checked by a senior diplomat before being "signed off". Particularly important dispatches must be checked by ambassadors themselves, since it is their name that goes at the end of the message (itself an unconscious reinforcement of the hierarchicalism of the system).

When you join the diplomatic service, you are instructed in the "house style" which strives for clarity, conciseness, detachment and, above all, objectivity. Drafting skill is highly rated. Some ambassadors become known for writing particularly well-crafted and witty missives and the best telegrams are circulated widely on an informal network as a kind of salute to the author.

But the telegram is also the embodiment of what diplomacy is about. In the British service, it is divided into Summary: a few lines; Detail: the main body of reportage; and finally the all-important Comment: what the embassy thinks of what is being reported and what policy they recommend to London. Thus a telegram may read something like this:

```
Immediate
To: FCO London
From: British Embassy Ruritaniaville
Classification: Confidential


Summary
1. Coup in Ruritania. An opportunity for the UK:
new President a good friend. No change recommended
for travel advice.


Detail
2. At 0200Z¹ today, a small band of army officers
led by General Potato seized the national radio
station, main army barracks and all principal
government buildings. There was a brief stand-off
at the presidential palace, but otherwise little
fighting and few casualties. Former president Tomato
has been imprisoned by Potato's men, who have
announced that he will be tried for corruption and
other "anti-state" crimes.
3. In a radio address at 0700Z, Potato declared
that the coup is for the "people of Ruritania"
to deliver them from the corruption and economic
chaos of the Tomato regime. While declaring himself
"transitional" President, Potato has announced
that there will be general elections within six
months or "as long as it takes for stability to be
restored".
4. The situation in Ruritania is generally calm.
Some demonstrators have come on to the streets to
```

celebrate the coup but otherwise there is little disturbance.

Comment
5. This coup has been brewing for some time (as other information has suggested).
6. While we [i.e. the UK] may disapprove of Potato's method of removing the government, Tomato's regime was a disaster for Ruritania, causing economic collapse and massive social unrest. Potato (whom I know well) has a level head and seems committed to the restoration of democratic government as soon as the security situation allows. We must insist that he keeps his word.
7. Potato's arrival offers an opportunity for us. I have dined privately with him frequently. Unlike Tomato, he is well-disposed towards the UK (he attended Oxford for one term). We should immediately re-examine our commercial and military export strategy.
8. We will keep the security situation under close review, but I see no need at present to alter our current travel advice.
    BACON [the surname of the ambassador]

Almost all such messages are classified from Restricted, the lowest level, up to Top Secret. The Foreign Office has succeeded in encouraging officials to downgrade the classification of many documents, for the more highly-classified a document, the greater the cost and awkwardness of circulating and storing it. However the vast bulk of such internal communications remain classified in some form. Thus a vast, effectively secret discourse is created.

Hundreds of such communications (though few of such drama) emanate from embassies all over the world every day. There is an unspoken, almost instinctive, understanding that the most impor-

tant parts of the world demand the most attention, so the British embassy in Washington, a huge office with many hundreds of officials, will send thousands of messages a year, while the two-person embassy in Ulan Bataar will only bother London a couple of times a month – or when there's a coup.

Historians may regard such written records as crucial manifestations of what is "really" going on inside a government — the core of its private deliberations. This is true, but only up to a point. In the crafting of these documents, to which diplomats devote considerable care, there are often distorting factors at play.

First, the documents are circulated widely in the foreign ministry and beyond, including to senior officials and ministers. They are thus, in the closed world of government, the most public demonstration of the skill and achievement of the author. This encourages all but the most unassuming ambassadors to play up the depth and intimacy of their political contacts: note (above) the fictional Bacon's emphasis on his close personal relationship with the new president. It is also worth remarking that this kind of analysis reinforces and perpetuates the view that governments — and the individuals comprising them — are the determining factors in international relations: that they are what really matters. The quality of relations with key local actors is the kind of thing which wins a big tick in the performance appraisal box when the ambassador is considered for promotion. Likewise, such telegrams will invariably stress the embassy's deep comprehension of the local scene. Never will they confess that they have little idea about what is going on.

I will here admit one shameful episode from my own career: when I was posted to Kabul, I was telephoned by the department in London and asked for a report on "the car bomb in Jalalabad". I

acknowledged the request and put down the phone. I had no idea what they were talking about. I duly went to the BBC website on the internet (whence presumably London had heard about it too), and took down a few details of the attack. Thus informed, I composed a short telegram back to London, classified it "restricted" and sent it.

Second, the division between "detail", i.e. fact, and "comment", i.e. judgement, in any such telegram implies such a separation in the mind and reporting of the ambassador. The separation makes sense in a system where readers need to know what is fact and what is opinion, but such a division belies the reality that the choice of what is reported at all implies a judgement in itself. Recall how in Bonn (chapter 2) my examination of the condition of the Roma did not justify a telegram. What embassies choose to report — what they see as a credible part of the discourse — is of course a judgement and a highly value-laden one at that.

Third, such telegrams are written to give the impression that they are offering considered and objective policy choices to the capital. When I was negotiating at the UN in New York, we would often in the "detail" (i.e. allegedly the "facts") section of the telegram describe the negotiations in such a way to persuade the reader (a senior official or a minister) of a particular course of action. For instance, if we in the mission disliked a proposal that London had asked us to put forward in a particular negotiation, we would often exaggerate in our reports the degree of opposition in order to encourage London to drop it. This was a subtle skill, but one in which we became very artful. I am sure we were not alone in this practice, though I doubt whether any serving diplomat will admit it. It would therefore be wrong to take such reports as fully accurate accounts of what they purport to be recording.

Finally, and perhaps most subtly, such communications do not necessarily communicate what the author really thinks. In my diplomatic career there are many telegrams I wrote that stand out in my memory. One commemorated the culmination of a year's gruelling negotiation to re-establish the UN Security Council's approach on Iraq (resolution 1284 (1999), which is I think the longest Security Council resolution of all time — see chapter 8); another, on 12 September 2001, reported the Council's condemnation of the attacks the day before. A third — in late 1998 — reported Iraq's promise of cooperation with the weapons inspectors, thus stopping the bombers which were already in the air from striking Iraq, although Iraq's promise was not fulfilled and the bombers nonetheless attacked later that year. I remember that when I composed this telegram, my hands were shaking so hard I could hardly type.

But one sticks out above all, not least because it was about an issue I have come to know very well, now from both sides of the table. The telegram was about the Western Sahara, one of the issues I was responsible for as head of the Middle East section at the UK Mission to the UN.

Few people have heard of this issue. Those who campaign about it argue that this is because the benighted people of Western Sahara (or Saharawis, as they are known) have never, unlike the Palestinians, resorted to terrorism. The Polisario, the organisation that represents the Saharawis, has never used violence as a political tool, except in direct resistance to the forces which occupy the Western Sahara in a guerrilla war which ended in 1991.[2]

The history is straightforward. When Spain, the colonial power, left the region known as Western Sahara in 1975, Morocco immediately invaded and occupied the territory. The inhabitants of the

region were offered no choice in this invasion, and their representatives, the Polisario, have ceaselessly campaigned for the Saharawis to be given the right to self-determination. In the early years, between 1975 and 1991, this campaign took the form of a sporadic guerrilla campaign. The Polisario decided to end the fighting in 1991 when the UN Security Council agreed a process, known as the Settlement Plan, whereby there would be a referendum in the territory on self-determination. Morocco threw up incessant obstacles to the plan's implementation. One of its techniques was to encourage Moroccan settlers in the territory to file thousands of objections to the voter registration lists prepared by the UN, thereby interminably delaying the preparations for the referendum. The Moroccans had also managed to convince their allies the French and US that if they lost the referendum, they would refuse to accept it.

In 2000, the UN Secretary-General appointed James Baker, the former US Secretary of State, as his Personal Representative on Western Sahara. His mandate, undeclared officially but unofficially understood by the permanent members of the Security Council, was to break this "deadlock" (a way of characterising the problem so that the main cause of it is absolved). In 2002 Baker offered three options to the Security Council: one to continue with the Settlement Plan, the second to offer the Saharawis a more limited autonomy (with the promise of a referendum on the territory's final status within five years) but under Moroccan sovereignty, and the third was to give up. The thrust of the recommendations — to abandon the Settlement Plan — was obvious: in other words, that the Security Council should abandon its own agreed approach to resolve the dispute simply because one of the parties was obstructing it.

In early 2000 the Foreign Office asked various of its embassies and missions, including New York, for their views on what "we" should do about Western Sahara. It fell to me to write the telegram from New York. My telegram duly reported what the UN Secretariat thought, what the French and US missions thought (notably, I did not seek the views of the Polisario representative, a charming and somewhat woebegone figure who ceaselessly tramped the corridors of the UN), and then what "we" thought. As was and is the practice, I divided the telegram into Summary, Detail and Comment. The Detail comprised my reports on what the UN, French and Americans had told me. These three actors had concluded that the Settlement Plan was running into trouble and that neither the US nor France was prepared to overcome Moroccan obstruction of the referendum. These were supposedly the "facts" on which I based my judgements, though, as I have noted, these facts did not include some details, such as the views of the Sahrawi representative, which to some might have seemed pertinent.

And just like our review of policy on Iraq sanctions, these "facts" did not include one word about the reality of life in Western Sahara for the Saharawis, Moroccans or indeed anybody else. I had never visited the Western Sahara. When eventually I did, in the autumn of 2005, I was appalled by the futility and suffering of some 150,000 Saharawi refugees who to this day remain in tented refugee camps in the western reaches of the Sahara, waiting for the "international community" to restore to them the justice they have been denied.[3] Having told "London" of the facts — which were merely the positions of the other "key" players — I then produced my judgement on what should be done about the Western Sahara problem. And here another deeply entrenched habit was put into play, namely

that of identifying, in an entirely arbitrary and subjective way, what were Britain's, or rather "our" interests in this affair. This is what the summary section of my telegram said:

"We should take a back seat: we have no dog in this fight."

Elsewhere, in the "Comment" section of the telegram, I wrote, "We have no national interest at stake", before recommending that we acquiesce, through quiet support, in the UN's impending decision to seek some alternative to the Settlement Plan and its referendum, an approach which we had many times endorsed and was supported in international law.

Why did I write this? I was, as a British diplomat of some ten years' experience, firmly gripped by a way of seeing the world which orders it in terms of states and their interests. From this perspective it was and is indeed the case that "Britain" had no national interest at stake in doing anything about the dispute. On the contrary, it had, by the traditional analysis, some measurable interest in *not* doing anything. Britain's exports to Morocco amounted in 2000 to some £402 million. Most of these exports were purchased directly by the Moroccan government and comprised armaments. For Britain to take a stand on the Western Sahara issue would have jeopardised that trade, particularly that with the government. So by this measure it was clearly in "our" interests to do nothing about Western Sahara.

What are our interests anyway, and how are they calculated? As elsewhere in the rarefied business of foreign policy, there is no "how to" guide or textbook to guide one. In the British Foreign Office, it is subliminally instilled into you that "our" interests generally consist of three things: trade, security and what are mysteriously called

"values". I have talked to many diplomats from other countries who tell me that their policies are based on similarly-termed analyses. In the British Foreign Office, we were not taught this calculus during our induction course, but it is something one infers from the endless disquisitions one subsequently reads where what "we" want is put into these terms. This is an arbitrary process. Very rarely are meetings held where ministers ask or even state what British "interests" are in any particular case. It is all pretty much assumed. Even to divide this amorphous set of interests into three subsets — trade, security and values — is to give a definition and rigour that this type of thinking rarely employs. Indeed, such is the subjectivity and arbitrariness of the components of foreign policy, that even to define them in this way is likely to be disputed. But for the sake of our own clarity of analysis, I must.

Economic "Interests"

Trade is the first obvious one. British trade with foreign countries is an easily measured variable. Such statistics appear in every annual review from embassies and in every analysis of bilateral relations with country x or y. These statistics give the trade factor a weight and psychological impact in any debate about policy. In the case of Western Sahara, my telegram put trade very much as *primus inter pares* in terms of our "interests", and I suspect that its statistical quality played a role. There is indeed some psychological research evidence which strongly suggests that people give more weight to clearly quantified data — numbers, percentages, etc.

It is assumed in places like the Foreign Office and in governments world-wide that trade is what their countries "want". But this of

course is a very big assumption. The foundation of this assumption is of course what underpins neo-classical economics, namely that individuals seek to maximise utility through consumption, i.e. people want more things. Writ on the national scale, this assumption is expressed as more trade and more growth. But there is growing evidence — and good, hard empirical data too — that this is not in fact the case.

At the most basic level — that of the individual — there is plenty of evidence to suggest that individuals are not primarily motivated by the desire to maximise their own wealth. For example, Professor (now Lord) Richard Layard has given a remarkable series of lectures (now a book[4]) showing that the pursuit of wealth has not made us any happier. Once people rise above a level of abject poverty, their level of happiness stagnates, despite increases in wealth. In the western world, the last fifty years have seen massive increases in wealth, but there has been no corresponding increase in happiness. The evidence he cites is not the nice, hard statistics of economics which have no measure of happiness, but psychology, where neuroscience has produced some compelling evidence in support of Layard's claims. Layard's assertions seem to be borne out by more global evidence. Global opinion surveys, such as those conducted by the Pew Center and Gallup International, suggest that while the escape from poverty is a primary global concern, other concerns, particularly once wealth levels rise, become more pressing.[5] These concerns, including things like crime, corruption and disease, do not fit easily, or even at all, into the assumptions of conventional economics on what motivates us.

This evidence fits in with well-established psychological theory about human needs and wants, such as Abraham Maslow's "hier-

archy of needs". This claimed that the highest level of human mo-
tivation was the need to achieve self-fulfillment. Below that were
other levels of need, each of which had to be satisfied before people
could progress to the next. At the bottom of Maslow's pyramid
of needs were the basics of life such as food, water and material
comforts. Next were safety and security needs. Then came love and
belongingness, including the desire to feel accepted by the family,
the community and colleagues at work. After that came the need
for esteem — both self-esteem and other people's respect and ad-
miration. Then finally, at the top, came what Maslow called self-
actualisation — the point at which people achieved the happiness
that came from becoming all they were capable of becoming. At this
level people might seek knowledge and aesthetic experiences for
themselves and help others to achieve self-fulfillment.

The measurement of happiness is inevitably a messier business
than that of, say, GDP. But the evidence clearly suggests that
Maslow's hierarchy is in operation. The poorest are least happy; the
better off generally more happy. But once a certain basic level of
income is reached, which may only be as little as $10,000 per head
per year, then levels of happiness stabilise. Increases in income and
wealth do not subsequently trigger increases in happiness. In fact,
levels of happiness can even decline.

This insight, which is occurring to more and more economists,
suggests many consequences. One is that the well-being of the world
would be increased by greater redistribution from rich to poor, as
the poor benefit from increases in income much more than the rich
do. But it also suggests that the central objective of governments in
the richer countries — the endless campaign to maximise national
wealth — may be the wrong one.

Taken to its fullest extent, this would mean a fundamental reorganisation of conventional political and economic thought. But at a minimum, it would suggest that the conventional assumption of foreign policy does not stand up: that a core "interest" of any particular country is exports and the maximasation of national growth.

Security "Interests"

Let us now look at the second great set of "interests" which states are commonly assumed to represent. This set is usually presented as a responsibility: to provide for the security of a state's citizens. This is such a widely-accepted norm of what states are meant to do that it has become an axiom, if not to say a tautology, of how we think about states and the world system: states exist to provide security for their citizens, ergo states must provide security for their citizens.

However, there is room to suppose that within this tautology there lies a self-perpetuating cycle. States exist to provide security. Therefore, in order for states to exist, they must ceaselessly prove that there are threats to their existence, thereby reaffirming their indispensability. The original reason why states exist, one is taught at most universities in the west, is to provide security for their citizens. Without the state, there is chaos. You will find this assumption everywhere in the core academic texts on foreign policy. In his essay "Perpetual Peace", Immanuel Kant repeats the assumption, routinely believed even in his day, that the state of nature — i.e. what the world would be like without states — is a perpetual one of war and lawlessness. Therefore the state is indispensable, and those who arbitrate what it wants are indispensable too.

One does not have to think too hard to realise that state élites have an interest (to use their terms) in making themselves indispensable, and to do so they must endlessly prove that the state is under threat. More dangerously still, they may actually behave in a way that encourages threats against the state. One way they do so is by emphasising the competitive or realist model of international affairs, a world of interacting and inevitably competing "interests". It's a dog-eat-dog world, they say. Eat or be eaten.

There are many examples of how government élites have exaggerated the threats against the state. During the Cold War the CIA overestimated the size of the Soviet economy and thus the resources that could be devoted to military production by at least a factor of two. More recently both the US and British governments exaggerated the extent of the threat posed by Iraq to the peoples of Britain and the US in order to fight a war that can only have been motivated by other reasons.[6] In this latter case, unable to prove an existential threat to their states themselves (even Saddam didn't have weapons capable of harming the US or British territories), both governments claimed that Iraq was a threat to their "interests". These were never clearly defined.

The exaggeration of threats is very much a function of the competitive, "realist" model of foreign policy thinking that is so pervasive today. To think in any other way — to claim, for instance, that economic and security "interests" may not be primary among a country's policy concerns — is instantly to exile oneself to the wildernesses outside policymaking circles.

If instead you are a member of a foreign policy élite – say in the British Foreign Office or the US National Security Council, or, in the US, one of the think-tanks staffed by the sort of people who

might end up in the NSC – you will already tend to think in the realist way (if you do not, your career in such places is likely to be short). The simplifications that you use to summarise what your state wants (usually unmodified by any relationship with the opinions of real people), prettifying these things by terming them as "interests", you will also tend to employ when thinking about other states: we want this; they want that. A model that inevitably emphasises competition, for only in a world of unlimited plenty can all wants be satisfied. The need for a clarity which any order requires inevitably encourages a tendency to polarise Us from Them. As Sartre once put it, we are defined by what we oppose.

The competition model is a deeply-rooted habit of thought and behaviour among nation states, clear even to those who are fresh to the scene. A relative newcomer to the world of international diplomacy is Luiz Inacio da Silva, the President of Brazil. Preparing to attend his meeting with the Group of Eight (G8) industrialised nations in June 2003, he commented on the leaders he would meet, "Politicians are like football coaches, they may like each other but they want their team to win. Chirac, Bush, Blair may like me but they're passionate about their own people".[7] In British newspapers, summits and international meetings are treated as diplomatic football matches, where success or failure is judged on the basis of whether We have got Our Way.

Values

This is an altogether more contested area of what should drive foreign policy. There are plenty of people who today contend that "values" is what British foreign policy is primarily "about" (you will

find such claims in the Foreign Office annual report or its website; such claims are repeatedly made in ministerial speeches). American leaders are even more forthright in claiming their mission to be the propagation of freedom, democracy and other American values. Some commentators go so far as to suggest that in this era of "post-modern" international order, values are a more important motor of foreign policy than more traditional indices of states' interests. This process parallels the evolution of supranational forms of organisation (the European Union is often given as the primary example), replacing the state as the principal unit of the international order.[8] Indeed, it is instilled in you from the very beginning of your career in the British foreign service that "British values" are what you are meant to represent. At first sight, these are simple things like democracy, accountability, the rule of law and open markets. More recently, the promotion of human rights has joined the list of "values" that "we" promote (at least in some places).

Before I joined the British Foreign Office, I had never given much thought to what British values were. Indeed, I would have thought it rather ridiculous to attempt to summarise them. This reservation had disappeared when, after about six years as a diplomat, I attended a conference of young British and European "opinion-formers" — journalists, trade unionists, civil servants and the like. It was not a very diverse group: there were no writers, painters or musicians and only a few people of colour. The predominant social designator was white, urban and middle class. Quite intentionally the conference was designed to reach "opinion-formers" — it was an élite.

The question arose: what were British values? Already steeped in the uncritical complacency of the government view of the world, I ventured an answer: decency, tolerance (I do not recall, thank God,

that I said "fair play" but I could easily have done). I naïvely thought that this description would kick off a friendly consensual discussion but instead my description was vehemently denounced by another participant. He used words like élitist, arrogant and short-sighted. My critic was a white, thirty-something policeman with cropped hair whose beat was where I had been born, Lewisham in South London. This example simply illustrates that there is little consensus on what British values are. More problematic still is how you prioritise and weight them: above all, how you pursue them.

In his essay "The Pursuit of the Ideal", Isaiah Berlin gives a measured yet devastating critique of all those who pursue absolutist, ideal solutions to the problems of mankind. He concludes that in deciding what to do, the only option, in private life as in public policy, is to engage in trade-offs: rules, values, principles must yield to each other in varying degrees in specific situations, adding that "a certain humility in these matters is very necessary" since we have no guarantee that any particular course we choose will be right.

One will rarely find such care among international policymakers. Rare now are the diplomats or political leaders who will claim their motives as purely selfish. Everyone now claims that "values" — whether they are imposition of democracy or the preservation of peace (the ubiquitous motive of "security") — are the motive. The Foreign Office is no different. In policy submissions and telegrams offering views on what to do about a particular situation, one will almost invariably find references to democracy, human rights or another "value".

It is, I suppose, a good thing that values are now reified to a higher place in the hierarchy of "interests", though I question whether "values" have not simply become a more palatable and politically-

correct excuse for realist "business as usual". The trouble is that the absence of consensus on what values are important or even what those values signify has given rise to enormous confusion. Relatively simple concepts like "democracy" are open to discussion about whether certain types of representation are more or less democratic than others. When it comes to concepts like "freedom", meanings are even more contested. Throw into the mix other vague objectives like "stability" and "security" and you can get very confused about which is more important than the other and even what these terms actually mean.

The result is, as Humpty Dumpty said to Alice: "when I use a word, it means just what I choose it to mean, neither more nor less". This translates to a total reliance, in places like the Foreign Office, on highly subjective judgements of what values are and which priorities to adopt. Although, like most people, I prefer to believe that I am a moral person, I have nevertheless many times lied and cheated in the name of British diplomacy, which is in theory supposed to represent "British values". Now that I have left the Foreign Office I do not make any claim to know what the values of the British people are. I doubt whether anybody else *can* have such an idea. We may talk about things like democracy, fairness and decency, and I would agree that these are things that many people in Britain think are important. But I would not *know*. Ask others outside Britain about what they think British values are and they are likely to offer a more discomfiting view. Bosnian Muslims will present a rather different answer from the one I gave at the conference. For that matter, why not ask British Muslims? But of course no one in British diplomacy ever does ask anyone else, least of all the people they are supposed

to represent, what British values are.[9] From the first day they enter the office, they are encouraged to believe that they know.

Economic interests, security interests and values are the three ingredients that generally make up the subjective mix of assumptions that underpin foreign policy calculations, even in relatively open and democratic countries like Britain.

And it was this type of analysis that British policy on Western Sahara adopted both before and since my involvement in the subject. The diplomatic situation has changed not one iota since then: there is still scant prospect of a referendum, and zero pressure, from the UN or its members, on Morocco to have one. The Saharawi refugees remain in their camps. In this case "values" do not make much of an appearance in the calculus, although I suspect that a close reading of the files (when they are opened in thirty years' time) will reveal that values such as "realism" and "pragmatism" are given prominence in the internal policy analyses. In the case of Western Sahara, the more traditional interests of trade and security point heavily in the direction of not standing up to the Moroccan government. British trade may be jeopardised by doing so. Meanwhile, the Moroccan government has become one of Britain's supposed "allies" in the "war against terrorism", i.e. by helpfully locking up Islamist terrorist "suspects" usually without trial or access to lawyers, according to Amnesty International.[10] Thus our security "interest" is reinforced; this is also true of the US, which has reportedly sent terrorist suspects to Morocco for interrogation in the programme known as "extraordinary rendition". Clearly in this case our "values" are not held sufficiently strongly to trump the other two sets of interests.

I thought I was being rather clever in putting this blunt example of *realpolitik* in the form "we have no dog in this fight." These were, infamously, the words used by James Baker in 1992 to declare that the US had no interest in intervening in the war in the collapsing state of Yugoslavia. My phrase was meant as an ironic echo of his, but if there was irony in my choice of words, the joke was on me because the telegram betrayed a deep and unconscious cynicism not only about British foreign policy, but about myself.

Looking back, this moment represents the triumph of the "we" over the "I" of me, the instant when my own personal values were subsumed and annihilated by the groupthink of "British national interests". If you had asked me then and now what I think about the Western Sahara issue, I would say that a great injustice was being done to the Saharawi people and that their rights was being ignored because no country was prepared to sacrifice its "interests" by putting real pressure on Morocco to grant the Saharawis their right to self-determination. But this is not what my telegram said; instead I wrote "we have no dog in this fight". My bosses approved the telegram and off it went to London, so they clearly agreed with me. And telegrams from other embassies and missions said more or less the same thing. If I had written that the Saharawis were being screwed sideways and something should be done, I have little doubt that my draft would have been returned to me with the comment that I should be more "realistic" or "less emotional".

What is bizarre and troubling about the episode is that most of my colleagues, and certainly those who dealt with Western Sahara at the Mission, all felt that a horrible injustice was being done. Our personal sympathies were very much with the Saharawis. We would say so to each other whenever we discussed the issue. Indeed, in

later years, the UN envoy dealing with the matter told me that most diplomats he talked to felt the same way. But none of us said so in our official telegrams, minutes and letters. Somehow we felt that to do so would be "naïve" or "not done". Our selves had been subsumed into a broader identity, one that had very little to do with what we each thought but with what we all thought we ought to think.[11]

I have often wondered since then who "we" were to make such judgements about what "Britain" wanted. If even the diplomats involved felt that an injustice was being ignored, what about "ordinary" British people? Would their reaction be that exports were more important than large-scale human misery? The truth is that I do not know. I certainly didn't know when I wrote the telegram saying what I thought "our" interests were. The British people were never consulted and they never will be.

In theory popular wishes are mediated through parliament where MPs are supposed to hold ministers to account. But the conflictual nature of the House of Commons, like Congress, encourages all parties to focus on those most contentious issues — Iraq, the Euro — rather than on other less fashionable cases like Western Sahara. Rare is the MP who knows about Western Sahara, rarer still the one who raises it in the House or writes letters to ministers. If an MP does raise Western Sahara, he or she will be given a sensible-sounding but very much a stock answer by the minister,[12] prepared by a desk officer like me. If they're lucky there might be an opportunity for a brief follow-up question, but that is all. Yet the UK's role as a permanent member of the Security Council is important and has the potential to be crucial, if only it would use it (I now speak as the frustrated campaigner, rather than the cynical insider). In the

US the Western Sahara is barely discussed at all, despite America's enormous potential to influence Morocco.

Take away this democratic input, and it is left to officials more or less to make up what they think "our" policy should be. Ministers of course take the decisions, and theirs is the ultimate responsibility, but the choices they are presented with are invariably premised on exactly the kind of thinking that I have described, i.e. a calculus of what "we", the state, want, based on an assessment — invariably subjective — of what those "interests" are. The suffering of the Saharawis is not ignored, and I assume that it concerns both the officials and ministers involved, but it is not given the weight of other factors.

The lesson here is obvious and depressing. For the Saharawis it is not enough to have right on their side and enjoy the personal sympathies of those who deal diplomatically with their situation. Somehow they must register on the scale of what matters to states, "interests" and *realpolitik*. It would be little wonder therefore if groups like theirs (but notably not them, yet), marginalised in the conventional discourse of what foreign policy should be about, were to resort to more violent methods to get noticed.

7

THE AMBASSADOR

The moral limits of the diplomat and "going too far"

"You cannot think without abstractions; accordingly, it is of the utmost importance to be vigilant in critically revising your *modes* of abstraction. It is here that philosophy finds its niche as essential to the healthy progress of society. It is the critique of abstractions. A civilisation which cannot burst through its current abstractions is doomed to sterility after a very limited period of progress."

Alfred Whitehead, *Science and the Modern World*

"You must realise this: that a prince and especially a new prince cannot observe all those things which give men a reputation for virtue, because in order to maintain his state he is often forced to act in defiance of good faith, of charity, of kindness, of religion. And so he should have a flexible disposition, varying as fortune and circumstances dictate."

Machiavelli, *The Prince*

(After Machiavelli...)

The ambassador is at the summit of his career.[1] *These are the days for which he has been preparing all his life. He has been honoured by his country, with*

medals and titles, and doubtless will receive more before he retires. People call him Sir, unbidden.

His clothing is elegant, understated but projecting a style of his type. Dark, well-cut, his suits hang well on him, as they are tailored to. His shirts are pressed and without wrinkle. His collars are clean and crisp. His tie is colourful, but never idiosyncratic. His socks have no holes, though they may, in a flash of self-expression, occasionally be red.

His demeanour is friendly but grave. His expression says that he is a man to be taken seriously: he has much on his mind. He may frown but he will never grimace. He may raise his voice, but he will never shout. Measure is his mien. In all things, measure.

The ambassador is the apotheosis of the diplomat. The young diplomat may be exuberant, may laugh and shout (occasionally); the ambassador, never. In the years leading to this point, the ambassador has learned to hold any emotion in check and to articulate what he has to say precisely and efficiently. Few words are wasted, except when many words are needed.

He is above all professional. I watch him as he chairs meetings of other diplomats. He is careful to show that he listens, nodding when others speak, acknowledging what they say when they have finished. When it is his turn to speak, he does so with a soft voice; it helps that his voice is deep. People listen.

If he disagrees, he says "I disagree," not "You are wrong." He never gives anyone a reason to dislike him, or to complain that he has wronged them. Personal difference cannot be allowed to intrude into business. He is charming and polite, though you can never really tell whether he likes you, or anyone else.

He is a successful diplomat. He is the vessel for his nation's wishes. He has travelled the world, lived in many of its countries. He can say hello and how are you in about six different languages. Maybe more, no one is ever sure.

I have been with him for many days and nights of hard diplomacy, of discussion of war and peace. I have watched and tried to know him, but have never succeeded. One night we went to war and for the first time I saw in him a kind of excitement. His eyes glittered as we watched the television with its images of explosions and the bombers that caused them. But that was the only time. Otherwise, a wry smile might be all you see of the man beneath. And what signifies the smile, no one can tell, perhaps not even him.

The stuff that we work on together is of infinite moment and importance. On our work rests the lives of many, sometimes conflict and sometimes peace. Great issues are at stake, of freedom, of democracy, of rights and human suffering. But while I am in turmoil and a frenzy of doubt and questions, he is serene.

I envy his serenity and for a time thought it a sign of great wisdom.

His government gives him a large and expensive car, and a driver, to whom he is always polite. The car carries a flag on some special occasions. He lives in a huge house, where servants prepare his meals and make his bed. Though magnificent, the house is not his. Its style is generic, designed "not to offend". A panoply of historic prints and tasteful wallpaper, it conveys no personality, for there is none behind it. No single mind has designed it. No one loves this house, since for no one is it a home.

The house sees an endless procession of guests. Official guests come from the home country to visit "abroad". A ceaseless round of receptions, lunches and dinners is held there. The waiters are discreet and courteous, and know how to serve a good wine, though it is never the best (government spending being what it is). The food is good, but never great. The furniture is attractive, but not splendid. It must serve a thousand guests, after all. And after a few years of use, it will be replaced, like the ambassador.

The ambassador's office is the embassy. Some embassies are exquisite, some are ugly. But wherever they are in the world, they carry the air of the home country within them. Pictures of the Queen adorn their walls. The

corridors ring with accents of home; discussions of the latest soap-opera or football game caught on satellite television. The ambassador's office is a little different from his staff's. It is larger, and has comfortable sofas on which to seat his many guests. There is the silence of an important place: the chatter and tickering keyboards of his secretaries are banished to an ante-room outside. If you visit, you will quickly be offered tea.

There is nothing like a war to help map the moral limits of those who work on it.

Iraq invaded Kuwait in the summer of 1990. One afternoon, as the coalition prepared to retake Kuwait, I was telephoned at my sleepy West European desk and summoned to join the war effort. The office needed staff to run the political-military liaison unit in what was called the Emergency Unit. The Emergency Unit was located in a special suite of offices underneath Whitehall. Quite why it needed to be situated down there was never clear to me, since there was no threat of Iraqi Scud missiles destroying the offices above ground. The absence of natural light and the necessary descent through combination-locked doors to the rooms certainly contributed to the sense of "emergency" and drama. The head of the unit did his bit to heighten the feeling of disorientation and crisis by immediately instituting a shift system of twelve hours on duty and twenty-four off (the unit had to be manned twenty-four hours a day). Thus within about two days of starting work, our sleep patterns were totally disrupted, we were exhausted and, on leaving the unit to emerge on to the streets above, we would never know whether it should be night or day.

My job consisted of sitting in a small office and reading reams of intelligence reports and summarising them for senior officials and ministers. Naturally, this was fascinating, though I soon learned that there is little information with a scantier connection to reality than "intelligence" information. I would often read blood-curdling reports of the imminent use of nuclear weapons — I remember one which gave a specific time for the launch of the nuclear-tipped missile — or the torture of British POWs (one supposed eye-witness report stated that captured British pilots had been dragged in chains by a pick-up truck through the streets of Basra, something which thankfully never happened). I would relay this to my seniors and they would say things like, "thank you, very useful" although I was never told what this information was useful for, and, looking back, I suspect it was not useful at all since the Foreign Office was not at all involved in the military prosecution of the war.

I had other tasks. Before the war, each bleary-eyed shift in the Pol-Mil Unit, as we were known, had been given instructions on what to do once the operation to retake Kuwait began. We were to be telephoned by a senior official who would give us a password —"Mikado"— and a time at which operations were due to begin (if Iraqi intelligence had been bugging our phones perhaps they were supposed to think that we were opera buffs). On receipt of the password, we were to telephone each member of the British Cabinet to inform them.

So it came about that one January night I was on duty with another officer. It was a regular evening without much to do. We had eaten the revolting food provided for our supper and were settling in for another night of watching television. Suddenly, CNN began to report explosions and gunfire in Baghdad. How exciting,

we thought, perhaps it's a coup, since no one had called us with the password. This went on for about half an hour until eventually the phone rang. "Mikado", said the disembodied voice, adding a time which was some thirty minutes later. And we then rushed about to call the Cabinet. I remember watching my fingers shake so much that I could not press the buttons on the telephone. I put on my most serious Foreign Office voice to say, "Minister, this is the Foreign Office Emergency Unit. Operations to retake Kuwait have begun." Most of them politely thanked us. One said, "Thank you, I know, I am already watching it on television."

There was a large room of the Emergency Unit filled with banks of telephones for consular calls, i.e. for ordinary people, whether in trouble or merely worried. In order to maintain surprise, none of its staff had been told that hostilities were to begin that night (indeed none of us had been told except Mikado). So no one was on duty. We rushed into the room. Every telephone was ringing furiously. On the wall was a counter showing the number of unanswered calls. Its digits were racing like a stopwatch. At random, I picked up a telephone. An hysterical woman screamed "Get my husband out of there!", meaning Saudi Arabia or somewhere else in the Gulf. Another phone, the same thing. I asked the head of the unit what the advice should be to these callers. He replied, "The official advice is 'Keep Your Heads Down'". I offered this to various of the panicked callers. It did little to calm them.

The war added a glamour to my private existence. I had to carry a beeper which I would ostentatiously parade at social occasions ("just in case I'm needed at the Foreign Office" I would say self-importantly if someone, as I hoped, noticed it). I would emerge from a night shift into a grey Whitehall dawn feeling somehow part of the

great scenery of "history". And indeed in a minuscule way I was. There had been reports that Allied bombers had damaged Shi'ism's most holy sites at Najaf and Kerbala. I wrote a press line about how every care was taken by our aircraft to avoid damaging sites of "cultural sensitivity". It was a convincing, well-crafted piece of text. The only thing to note about it was that I had no idea whether "our" aircraft were taking such care. I certainly didn't ask the Royal Air Force people in London, let alone in the region. I assumed they were, but for all I actually *knew* they could have been directing their bombs on to the very tomb of Imam Hussein himself. Yet I wrote the press line, and it was used with considerable conviction by both our ministers and indeed by Colin Powell.

Buried in our bunker, I learned and practised the arts of propaganda. Before the war began, the Allied governments talked up the awfulness of the Iraqi threat. I calculated that Iraq had more main battle tanks than all the armies of Western Europe combined (as long as you counted them in a particular way). One of our Ministers (it might even have been the Prime Minister) said that the Iraqi army was the third largest in the world. Some journalists had queried this claim. I was therefore tasked to "prove" this statement. I duly consulted *Jane's Armies of the World* and performed the necessary calculations. I could only "prove" the Prime Minister's assertion by including Iraq's enormous reserve forces (which amounted to over a million) and ignoring the reserves of the other contenders for the third-largest spot. But I need not have worried. The "fact" that Iraq had the third largest forces in the world had become one of those factoids, believed by almost everyone (except those who bothered to read the books), validated merely by multiple repetition.

Operation Desert Storm proceeded. Some members of my unit pasted large maps on the walls of our subterranean offices, showing the dispositions of our and the Iraqi forces. As the intelligence came in — or as CNN reported movements — they would move little flags and symbols up and down the maps. You could tell that they loved doing it because we had no need for the maps as we were not involved in any way with actual military operations. It reminded me of the fun I had playing wargames at school, massing Russian divisions, symbolised with little cardboard hexagons, against the Germans on the Eastern Front on a large boardmap of Europe. I had my own duties. Behind my desk was a row of old-fashioned bakelite telephones. Occasionally one would ring and it was my job to answer it. A voice would say "A scud [missile] has been launched towards Dhahran [or Tel Aviv or wherever]". I would say "thank you very much" and replace the receiver. I would then announce to the unit that a Scud had been launched towards Tel Aviv and we would all turn on CNN to see shots of people frantically putting on gas masks in Tel Aviv. There was no other purpose for the telephone calls.

Although there was an undoubted excitement to these moments, there was also something terrible about them. We had seen plenty of information, from a variety of sources, suggesting that Iraq would use chemical, biological or even nuclear weapons. We never knew if this Scud launch might be the one that would bring hideous destruction with it. One night I read a report indicating a specific time when Iraq would launch a nuclear-tipped missile towards Israel. It was a tense night. But, I don't care to admit, there was also something "real" about it, even though we were experiencing the war only remotely. There was a verve and punch to those days. The eyes of the officials in the unit, despite the strange hours we worked,

were alive and sparkling. People loved to work on the war. Staff would come in to the unit even when they weren't on duty. There was no work for them to do (truth be told, there was often very little for any of us to do), but they clearly wanted to be part of the "action". One senior official made a fetish of coming to work and announcing to all about how his marriage was collapsing or he was missing his daughter's birthday because of his work, yet he didn't need to be there. There was a ghastly machismo about it. I remember us all having a good manly guffaw at the news that only one of the five bombers the pathetic Italians sent had managed to reach its target.

All of the officials in that rabbit warren of offices, including me, would say then, and perhaps now, that it was all terribly serious, but I suspect that many would know in their deepest senses that they enjoyed it. There is nothing like the excitement of war, particularly one where you yourself are at no risk whatsoever.

At the same time as I began, in a somewhat scattered and incoherent way, to realise why people, especially men, are driven towards the excitement of conflict (as I was too), I also became aware of a strange disconnection. One night, a British Tornado pilot was interviewed on the television. Asked what he thought of the rightness or wrongness of what he was doing, he replied that he simply did what the "politicians" wanted. He added that he did not have time to think about the "whys and wherefores", as he put them – he just did his job. I pondered this statement and realised that we officials too, though in a less pointed fashion than the man who actually dropped the bombs, were in the same position. Although we were involved in the enterprise of war, none of us seemed to feel any real sense of responsibility for it.

I thought about this during the 2003 war with Iraq, when British officials (by that time my former colleagues) would tell me that they thoroughly disagreed with the war, even though — they did not add — they were thoroughly involved in executing it too. The ultimate conclusion of this logic is that only the ministers who decide to engage in a war are morally responsible for it.

There are reasons to question this comfortable assumption. Such a logic runs counter to the evolution of international law which, since the Nuremberg Trials, has emphasised that "obeying orders" is not a legitimate defence. This is not to suggest that our various wars with Iraq involved war crimes, but instead to point out the inconsistency of the logic which many government and military people seem to adhere to. For, whether bomber pilot or backroom official, we were all of us actively involved in the enterprise: the material facts of our actions could not be denied.

The argument of the pilot, which I think would have been shared by many if not all of the officials I worked with, is as follows. War is decided by "the politicians"; they are accountable through parliament; we — the functionaries — do what the politicians tell us. Our accountability is to them. We have no wider moral accountability. This reasoning fails some fundamental moral tests, such as Kant's belief that you are morally responsible only for that which you can control. (For the more religious, God sees everything we do.) For the pilot and the official both have control in that they can choose not to participate. They are not forced to collaborate in policy. They can resign. There may be penalties for doing so, but they do nonetheless have that choice. This objection notwithstanding, the belief, whether rationally articulated or believed in some

less coherent, emotional way, is widespread in government service. We just do what we are told.

The powerful and dangerous consequence of this mental habit is that it contributes to an undoubted moral numbness, although it felt not like numbness in the Gulf War Emergency Unit, but like complete indifference. It simply wasn't our job to worry about the moral implications of what we were doing. To believe so would have been seen as hopelessly naïve. I have noticed the phenomenon particularly among some senior officials, whose sensibilities have been blunted by years of experience. The moral limits of the "system", of "politics", have become their own moral limits, so that they exhibit no separation between their own personal moral sphere and that of the political system in which they are working. Moral ugliness is breezily dismissed, "that's just politics/the way the world is/the system, get over it." Worse, this moral indifference is presented as a virtue: that those like them who see things as they "really are" are the more "practical" and "realistic". Those who dare to exhibit their own moral judgement or criticism are condemned as "romantic", "sentimental" or just plain "immature".

There is a particular sobriquet that attaches itself to those who exhibit their moral sensibility too often or too openly, one which speaks also of the unspoken, class-derived norms of Foreign Office manners, that of "going too far". In the 1990s there was one particular senior ambassador to a large Middle Eastern country who, it was felt, was "going too far". He would send telegrams to London suggesting that Western policy in the Middle East was iniquitous: the Palestinians were being treated terribly and the Israelis should be more harshly censured. And he would say this quite often. For this expression of views, it was said in the Foreign Office (phone

calls among colleagues, office gossip, muttered asides at meetings) that Sir X had "gone too far", that he had abandoned that fabled quality: "balance". Occasionally, I too was called to order in my performance reports for "going too far". Debating at a staff dinner in Bonn, I had attacked a colleague for his defence of Britain's inaction to prevent the Holocaust in World War Two. This, my report said, showed a tendency to "go too far". My performance rating was duly downgraded.

One important point to notice about both these examples is that the tendency to "go too far" was in both cases exhibited in private, within the confines of the Foreign Office's walls. I have little doubt that the senior ambassador did his job and was duly loyal to government policy when he was in foreign company, just as I was in pursuing what "we" wanted in my official work. But "going too far" was nonetheless condemned as a dangerous character flaw.

It only slowly became clear to me where the boundary lay between "balance" and "going too far". "Balance" lay in never questioning the broad thrust of what "we" wanted or were doing. One was entitled to question and debate small details, but suggesting, for example, that sanctions were morally wrong was very much "not done". Indeed, to mention that there should be a moral component to policy was regarded, in the unstated and inexplicit way that a culture operates, as naïve and unprofessional.

This was very much the culture of the *officials* in the Foreign Office. I always found that *ministers* (i.e. the politicians), by comparison, were much more willing to debate and hear criticism of the fundamentals of policy. I would have to seek them out in private, in order to avoid another "going too far" remark in my next personnel report, but whenever I did so, I invariably found them receptive.

This was paradoxical because I was told by my seniors on a tedious number of occasions that officials were not supposed to question what ministers wanted. In fact, I often found that ministers wanted us to do just that, provided it was in private.

Ministers seemed to show an instinctive understanding that policy was about something more than just the allegedly-empirical world of "facts" (however dubiously derived) like states, security and interests. For "going too far" in some ways represents crossing over into the non-empirical realm of morality. To remain "balanced" was to choose to remain in the world of the state system, the world as it is: a world of statistics, even invented ones like Iraq's third-largest army in the world, and cold-eyed "realism". To accept such a reductionist version of the world is to succumb to the worst kind of cynicism, where that cynicism is not even declared or admitted as such. Sometimes when I looked in the eyes of those senior officials I thought I saw a kind of death, that some part of their soul had shrivelled and died with disuse.

But at the time of the "Gulf War" such meditations were far in the future.[2] My interior moral debate did not prevent me from enjoying the exterior experience. Indeed it gave it a certain ambiguous drama.

To think that the state and its servants must embody a different morality from that of ordinary people is widespread in the world of diplomacy. It is an acceptance often expressed with weary cynicism or an indifferent shrug, "it is the way of the world": *realpolitik*. It is an idea whose antecedents stretch back into antiquity. Its most famous philosophical proponents are the Greek historian Thucydides, Machi-

avelli (most notably in *The Prince*) and Thomas Hobbes (in *Leviathan*). The more recent exponents of realism include Henry Kissinger and the former British Foreign Secretary Douglas Hurd, who infamously dismissed those who sought Western intervention in the Yugoslav meltdown as the "something-must-be-done brigade".[3]

In academic circles they are known as proponents of the "realist" view of international relations. For realists the laws governing politics have changed little if at all through the years. Although there are some differences between so-called neo-realists and classical realists, all theories of realism are sceptical of universal moral principles. The state, they argue, is by far the most important institution in international relations. They claim that collective action (for instance in the UN) is unlikely to work beyond short-term agreements, that a balance of power will emerge between rival alliances, and that war cannot be eradicated from international relations. *Raison d'état* governs the world.

I suppose my views represent more of what is known as the "liberal" view of international relations. Alongside realism, liberalism remains one of the predominant strands of Western political thought and practice. Like realism, liberalism has a rich heritage, encompassing such figures as John Locke, J.S. Mill, Jean-Jacques Rousseau and Immanuel Kant. Though difficult to generalise into one paradigm, it offers a more universalist approach — law, human rights — to international affairs. As liberalism evolved in the twentieth century (and some called it neo-liberalism), it argued that cooperation and collective security in a multipolar system of democratic states and strong international institutions would best serve the interests of stability (echoing Kant's "perpetual peace"). Many contemporary liberals viewed the end of the Cold War (the

realist paradigm of a bipolar system) as the ultimate confirmation of liberalism as the only viable mode of political life.

Champion among such thinkers was Francis Fukuyama who, in his seminal book *The End of History and the Last Man*, argued that political history had come to a close with the death of the Cold War and, by default, the triumph of liberalism. Not only will liberal democracy and capitalism spread through an ever-globalising world, but also such a system would be ideal. A world wherein all states adhere to liberal democratic norms, institutions and universal political values would be one that neutralises war and conflict. From Kant onwards, liberals embraced the idea that representative democratic governments would never resort to violence because rational, free-thinking individuals would never consider war in their best interest. Additionally, growing economic interdependence means that states have increasingly higher stakes in ensuring mutual peace and prosperity.

Meanwhile, in the US, a new school of thought, neo-conservatism, emerged, which reflects elements of both realism and liberalism. Unlike the proponents of these other schools, the neo-cons are more policymakers and politicians than theorists. The most definitive exposition of neo-conservatism as a movement has been put forward by the Project for the New American Century, a think-tank whose statement of principles carries the names of Vice President Dick Cheney, former Vice President Dan Quayle, former Assistant Secretary of Defence and current World Bank President Paul Wolfowitz, former Secretary of Defence Donald Rumsfeld and another twenty-odd prominent American policymakers and academics.

In brief, contemporary neo-conservatives promote four key foreign policies: maintaining and expanding US military forces, openly challenging hostile regimes, promoting economic and political free-

dom and shaping the international order to one best fit for American "security, prosperity and principles". In short, neo-conservatives hold that the advancement of American goals and interests is important and beneficial not only for the US but for the rest of the world.

With some echoes of Woodrow Wilson's liberal idealism in promoting American ideals of government and economics abroad, neo-conservatives differ from other conservatives with their aggressive and moralist foreign policy stance. (Many neo-cons for instance, although not in government at the time, supported the decidedly anti-realist position that the US should intervene to stop Serb ethnic cleansing and seizure of territory during the Yugoslav wars.) That neo-conservatism draws on the ideas of Wilson indicates the ideological diversity within the movement. Indeed, many neo-conservatives once affiliated themselves with liberal or even far-left political ideologies; many considered themselves neo-conservative in the past but are no longer. Apart from their common interests in foreign policy, neo-conservatives are almost universally united in their opposition to communism. The "War on Terror" and the "Bush doctrine" show the significant influence of the "neo-cons" on American policy today.

In any debate on foreign policy, you will observe these strands emerge: morality *vs raison d'état*; intervention *vs* persuasion and non-military coercion; confrontation *vs* negotiation or cooperation. Added to the mix is the dichotomy of soft *vs* hard power, an idea (originated by Harvard professor Joseph Nye) that power has many expressions other than military force, including cultural and institutional persuasion. As Nye himself says,

"The basic concept of power is the ability to influence others to get them to do what you want. There are three major ways to do that: one is to threaten them with sticks; the second is to pay them with carrots; the third is to attract or co-opt them, so that they want what you want. If you can get others to be attracted, to want what you want, it costs you much less in carrots and sticks."

The contrast is often made between the "soft power" of the European Union, which encourages states to behave better through the carrot of EU membership or other EU-granted advantages, and the "hard" militaristic approach of the Bush administration.

These theories were developed to help explain international relations, and in some cases — the neo-cons being the most recent example — to help shape policy. Looking back at my experience of policymaking and implementing foreign policy, I find however that their relevance is limited. I have argued in earlier chapters that realist concepts still play a large role in shaping how diplomats think about the world — states identifying their interests and interacting, and sometimes fighting, on the basis of these interests. Liberal ideas of projecting universal values — rights and law — also have an influence, to a greater or lesser degree depending on the circumstance. But the very coherence and neatness of these theoretical explanations of diplomatic behaviour betrays the reality, and the complexity, of what actually took place.

In government, officials tend to think in a "realist" manner, defining their interests and choices according to *realpolitik*. While I have argued that such thinking is still far too dominant in policy-making, there is also a substantial "liberal" sentiment at play too (and this was true of Conservative as well as Labour governments in Britain,

Republicans and Democrats in the US): that we should be driven by more universal concerns for human rights and the diminishing of suffering. There can be no doubt that neo-conservative ideas played a substantial part in driving the US decision to invade Iraq in 2003, but as I have discussed in chapter 4, they cannot have been the only factor. There were doubtless many others at play. Only in newspaper columns is the argument put into simple dichotomies.

What one finds in the world of diplomacy today is rarely distinguishable into these theoretical boxes. Policymakers are influenced by a mass of different factors, some historical, some cultural, some emotional and some indefinable. To pretend that decision-makers or policy-framers look at the world in terms of theory (whether liberal or realist) is dangerously reductionist. The more subtle and complex reality I experienced suggests a certain scepticism about the explanatory utility of these theories. In short, policymaking is more random, more arbitrary, just simply messier and more human than theory would have us believe.

(One consequence of this reality is, again, to underline the requirement for greater scrutiny of those within the system. For if decision-making is as arbitrary and unsystematic as I claim, then all the greater is the power of those within the system — since they are not following a consistent theory — and thus greater the need to query and check their actions.)

This is understandable. Foreign ministers and diplomats are human after all. But the desire to fit real events into these conceptual structures often diminishes, not increases, our understanding. NATO's intervention in Kosovo is often presented as a pivotal moment in the evolution of the doctrine of "humanitarian intervention", namely the idea that states can intervene in other states,

against their governments' will, in order to protect civilians against genocide or widespread oppression. This right is not yet incorporated into international law.

But NATO's intervention was driven by many factors, including guilt over its failure to prevent genocide in Bosnia and in particular the Srebrenica massacre. Other factors included the fact that the majority in Kosovo (the Kosovo-Albanians) were being so clearly repressed by Milosevic's Belgrade, the power of the almost real-time imagery of Kosovo refugees being driven from their country, the diplomatic isolation of Milosevic and the sense that he was near the end of his power, the overwhelming military superiority of NATO which allowed intervention without risking Western troops on the ground, the power of the pro-Albanian lobby in the US, the role of the UN Security Council and international law (the Council neither endorsed nor condemned the intervention), the idea that the West could not admit more chaos and genocide in Europe (though it was ready to allow it in Africa), and of course the personal inclinations of the leaders concerned which must perforce have comprised their own private narratives of the meaning of morality, history, the nation state and their own emotional motors. This combination of factors came to a head at a particular moment in 1999 and pushed the decision-makers towards intervention. Had the crisis arisen in 1996 or 2002, it is hard to believe that they would have made the same decision. And even this account is inevitably simplistic.

It seems to be something intrinsic to discussion of foreign relations that we tend to conceptualise in such generalised terms. When Machiavelli was writing about international relations, his world was divided into states which traded and occasionally went to war with one another, but that was about all, and their trade

and other interactions were but a tiny proportion of their total economic and other activity. It is a very different story today where the interactions of states (with the exception of a few isolated hermits like North Korea) are massive and heterogeneous. The world is not divisible. Hobbes's ideas were very much driven by the need to avoid civil war (which gripped England during his lifetime) not international war, yet his ideas of the state and the alternatives to it still influence basic, and often unspoken, assumptions about international relations.

One of the oddities of the discourse of international relations is that it treats the world of states and their doings as on a separate plane. It is as if states float above the realm of ordinary people and that therefore they require different forms of analysis and moral scrutiny. Perhaps this is because we are taught, by the inevitable simplifications of history, to regard states as separate entities, discrete and with agency. Perhaps our natural desire for order and patterns encourages us to do this too. History we prefer to see as a linear progression, indeed as "progress", until the present moment.[4] Like us, the world betrays little order, and as we advance into the twenty-first century, the neatness of past centuries (though were they ever really neat?) falls away, and we encounter something that looks more and more like entropy, disorder.

There is danger here too. The more complex the world becomes, the less it will respond to our simplistic models of how it should behave. The temptation will arise to make it respond. This is one way (and only one of many ways) of viewing the Bush Administration's invasion of Iraq (whose putative motivations are discussed at further length in chapter 4): it was an attempt, post the devastating ruction of 9/11, to reassert an American order

on the world, an order more reflective of the realist analysis of the 2001 National Security Council strategy document: a world of states and threats which must be countered. The post-invasion history of Iraq has shown how inappropriate that form of analysis is. As I write in 2006, the removal of a dictator has spawned not stability but chaos in a country that barely warrants such a designation, where many post-national (or pre-national) forces — religious, ethnic, anti-American, fundamentalist — are at play in a confusing and violent mêlée.

Thus to understand the world internationally today, we need more than the theory of how states behave. We need to understand that a state is a mere agglomeration of individuals, not a singularity. To understand these groups and their leaders, we must acknowledge their great complexity, and develop a debate about their moral behaviour in the international context (not deny its relevance). We must apply the tools with which we understand other forms of human behaviour, whether collective or individual: psychology, anthropology, and perhaps the more arcane means of interpreting hidden motives such as semiotics and even art. We must employ too our understanding of our physical space — the environment, natural resources — in order to accommodate its effects upon our behaviour and our lives. None of these factors is separable without artifice; even together, they lend themselves poorly to generic theorising. We must be humble before these many signals, and aware of the limits of our capacity to interpret them.

And while theory has its limits, even words and terms themselves sometimes cannot convey all that is important.

STAR TREK, WITTGENSTEIN AND
THE PROBLEM WITH FOREIGN POLICY

"Ever since men began in time, time and
Time again they met in parliaments,
Where, in due turn, letting the next man speak,
With mouthfuls of soft air they tried to stop
Themselves from ravening their talking throats;
Hoping enunciated airs would fall
With verisimilitude in different minds,
And bring some concord to those minds; soft air
Between the hatred dying animals
Monotonously bear toward themselves;
Only soft air to underwrite the in-
Built violence of being, to meld it to
Something more civil, rarer than true forgiveness.
No work was lovelier in history;
And nothing failed so often: knowing this
The army came to hear Achilles say:
'Pax Agamemnon.' And Agamemnon's: 'Pax'"[1]

*It's a regular Wednesday morning and here we are in one of the central
chambers of world diplomacy: The United Nations Security Council, where*

*nation shall speak unto nation. Here the discussion is of death and starva-
tion, of sanctions and nuclear weapons, of genocide and ceasefires. Here we
arbitrate war and peace; we ponder the fate of millions. We wield the power
of life and death in this place, the crucible of our modern secular world
order. Our business here could not be of greater import. And yet there is
something missing, something vital yet indefinable.*

*It has been a long morning. It's hot and stuffy. The chamber is too small
for the sixty or so people crammed inside it, arrayed in fifteen tight delegations around a flattened U-shaped table. Chairs fixed to the floor, like some
prison canteen, deepen the sense of confinement. The light is dismal. A few
stray beams of sunlight filter through the blinds drawn on the day outside.*

*Through uncomfortable plastic earpieces, the delegates listen distractedly
to the monotonous translations of the interpreters who sit behind them, separated in elevated booths, "…My delegation wishes to reiterate the need for
all parties to participate in the dialogue and to bring this dispute to a peaceful conclusion…". One by one the heads of the delegations intone the same
platitudes, the same words — states, security, peace, war, civilian casualties
— rolling off their tongues in a well-practised and repetitive litany. I'm
thinking about my date in the evening. I force myself to concentrate. It's
twelve-fifteen. We're halfway through the morning's agenda. That means
we must be discussing…genocide.*

*I hadn't thought the UN Security Council would be boring, but it is.
I sit, I take notes, I take more notes. I crave a cigarette. We and the other
diplomats in other delegations occasionally grin at one another or pass wit-
less jokes on scraps of paper. The day's agenda is the usual roster of unsolved
conflict and human misery: Burundi, Iraq, East Timor, Congo. The list is
a long one.*

*With each new agenda item, another intractable dispute. A map is pro-
jected on to a white screen at one end of the room. The UN Special Envoy
or Secretariat official is wheeled in to give the Council the state of play:*

"We regret to inform Council members that fighting has continued over the reporting period, with civilian casualties on both sides...". The ambassadors sitting at the front flick an eye of greeting and attempt to stay awake for the discussion to come. The diplomats at the rear of their delegations click their ballpoints and open their notebooks.

The junior diplomats in each delegation take the note, as it's known. It's a straightforward if demanding job. Most of the wars around the world have similar dimensions, as long as you describe them in a particular way. The attributes of conflict can be simplified in my notes. Lots of people dying becomes, "v.dead", mass starvation "v. starv", continuing conflict "cont. conf.", and so on.

The reports come and go; the maps flicker on and off. Now it's the densely-packed land of Rwanda, now it's Sierra Leone. I'm colour-blind so most of the maps look pretty monotone to me and I have to look closely to tell the difference. Maps were introduced at the proposal of one well-intentioned ambassador. The idea was to give delegations a better sense of the countries they were discussing. He didn't mean it as a joke.

The discussions come to an end and, with a sigh and a yawn, the delegations make their way out, the ambassadors to an expensive lunch at one of the many eateries of New York's midtown, the junior diplomats to a sandwich and back to the office to write up their reports. I wander out, smoke a cigarette, chat to other diplomats, maybe some journalists hanging about outside the chamber. I think about the report I have to write; I think about what I'm going to do that evening.

Somehow the cigarette smoke in my lungs, as I suck it deep down, is more real than anything we've been doing all morning. Here we are at a confluence of world affairs, and it doesn't seem real at all. The issues that we've been discussing — war, deprivation, genocide — are momentous and awful: people are dying as we speak. But somewhere along the way they have been made lifeless and denuded of all human content.

If you make an enormous effort of imagination, you can just about conjure up a picture of the human beings whose existence is at stake — the victims of genocide in Rwanda, the civilians massacred during a rebel advance in the Congo — but it is a stretch, and sooner or later you stop doing it because it's upsetting, tiring and, frankly, unnecessary. It's easier just to do what's necessary, write the report, negotiate the resolution, get home (our hours are long, even by the Stakhanovite standards of New York City). And slowly but surely you become deadened to it all. Wars, brutalities, peace plans, blah, blah, blah.

Though we were at the heart of things, we seemed to be missing the point. Terms — diplomatic words, statistics, resolutions — were our tools to arbitrate a world of blood and agony. We were dealing with reality but working in abstraction. Something was missing.

———————————

This something was not just absent in that airless room; it is an absence in the entire discourse of foreign policy. For the terms and manners of the diplomats in that chamber reflect those of the way in which foreign policy is practised — by statesmen and diplomats — and talked about — by journalists and academics — across the world. That little room was a microcosm.

The turmoil of recent years has brought attention to international affairs in a way unprecedented since perhaps the Cuban missile crisis or the darkest days of the Vietnam war. Living in New York City before September 11, few of my New York non-diplomat friends talked about foreign affairs; if they did, it was often in an academic, disinterested way. Since that dreadful day, one can hardly avoid it. The terms — multipolarity, containment — the names and acro-

nyms — WMD and GWOT — once only known to the insiders of foreign and security policy, have now become ubiquitous. But like thieves in the night, they have entered our world and discussion un-noticed and unquestioned. Time perhaps to examine the epistemology of diplomacy.

I was once briefly posted to Oslo. Despite the friendliness of the locals and my colleagues in the Embassy, I often had long hours to kill in the isolated bungalow in the outskirts of Oslo where I lived. I had no car and my bicycle, though equipped with fearsomely-spiked ice tyres, was inadequate to transport me in the snowy, dark Norwegian winter. To assuage my loneliness, my boss kindly lent me her large collection of episodes of *Star Trek: The Next Generation* (or simply "TNG" as it is known to the *cognoscenti*). She would give me a commentary on each episode, opening my eyes to the diplomatic morality tales hitherto undetected therein.

"This one's about Northern Ireland", she would say and indeed the episode concerned a planet where two communities had warred for millennia. It concluded when Commander Riker, the most American of the crew, declared: "Perhaps peace will come when the first child decides to put down his gun." There was one about Vietnam veterans, where a planet's inhabitants had banished a group of genetically-programmed warriors to an orbiting moon because they were unfit for peaceful society now that their fighting was done. That one ended with a little homily too.

The "TNG" character I liked least was Deanna Troi, the "empath" on the ship who, on approaching an alien planet, would close

her eyes, put her fingers to her forehead and say things like, "I am feeling much pain and unhappiness" — such feelings could not of course be detected by the *Enterprise*'s other sensors. She seemed to me to represent a kind of wishy-washy, psychobabbly approach to tackling aliens and resolving conflict. I preferred the harder, more analytical methods of Captain Picard, played, need it be said, by a narrow-eyed Englishman with a Shakespearean accent (though why does he have a French name?). Guns and treaties were the methods of intergalactic relations I liked, not feelings. If an episode was centred around Troi, I would stop the tape and find a more masculine episode ("Final battle with the Borg"). Such were my days in Oslo.

Unattractive though I found her, Counsellor Troi embodied an important insight into the nature of diplomacy (or space exploration, whichever you prefer). This was her ability to enter and interpret the realm beyond normal data-collecting tools. The Californian scriptwriters who dreamt her up may have been thinking merely of the emotional realm beyond conventional measure. But of course it is not merely the emotions that lie beyond the capacity of tools of description or measurement.

All tools of description, all terms and all language, are limited. No measurement, no depiction can ever quite capture the fullness of a phenomenon. It is impossible to describe what an experience, any experience, is actually like. Well, to be more accurate, one can say what it was *like*, but never what it *was*. My experience of drinking a cup of coffee is going to be quite *like* your experience of drinking a cup of coffee, but it is impossible for me to convey to you, however vivid and inventive the terms that I use, the *actual* experience. I could put the experience into scientific terms and describe the encounter of the heated water and coffee molecules with the nerve endings on

my tongue, then the stimulus of the caffeine chemicals upon my brain synapses and blood pressure. I could film the act of coffee drinking, or try to convey it in poetry or music. But whatever the medium, whichever terms I choose, there would always be an absence: the difference between description and the experience.

This much is obvious and familiar. Philosophers have long grappled with the relationship between description and reality. Ludwig Wittgenstein spent most of his philosophical energies exploring the connections between language and experience. In the only work published in his lifetime, *Tractatus Logico-Philosophicus*, he concluded with his famous near-tautology on the limits of language, "Whereof one cannot speak; thereof one must remain silent." From the preceding arguments of this strange and sometimes impenetrable book, one can conclude that he meant that while language has a logical structure, that logical structure cannot be described in language; it can only be *shown*. In other words, the relationship between words and reality cannot itself be put into words; it can only be demonstrated through the use of those words. Wittgenstein in *Tractatus* takes the argument further to claim that almost everything that is most important cannot be stated at all, but only, at the very most, *indicated* by our use of language.

In his later work Wittgenstein took a different tack — and a broader view of language — and emphasised the role of philosophy in scrutinising and clarifying the meaning of words through their usage. But, as Ray Monk describes in his excellent biography,[2] he never abandoned his identification of the limits of ordinary language. As he approached his death, he grew increasingly despairing of the reliance of contemporary society upon the seductive tools and terms of science to describe and arbitrate the world. He remained through-

out passionately committed to the importance of music, poetry and other non-scientific, indeed non-linguistic, forms of expression as revelatory of the human soul, of the human reality. Neither scientific terms nor words could ever be enough. As he says in *Tractatus*, "We feel that even when all scientific questions have been answered, the problems of life remain completely untouched. Of course then there are no questions left, and this itself is the answer."

The distinction between what is describable through words and other conventional descriptive tools and what is not brings us close to other ancient borders, that between the world of physical reality and the metaphysical, and between the rational and the irrational. Some might spot the same boundary between the testable certainties of science and the unprovable inexactnesses of the arts, though Heisenberg's uncertainty principle has perhaps undermined science's claim — which I suspect that few scientists believe in any case — to certain knowledge.

Mathematics has already, since Euclid, come to grips with the immeasurable. Indeed, the term irrational in mathematics means that which is not commensurate with ordinary numbers, something that cannot be put into finite numerical terms: literally, the unquantifiable.

That the unquantifiable exists therefore is unarguable, and speaks to our own intuition about our existence: there are simply some things that cannot be put into terms and perhaps, as Wittgenstein argued, these are the most important. The trouble with foreign policy, however, is that there is no acknowledgement, least of all reckoning (if such a thing is possible), of this truth. This deficit is one that is shared in all policymaking, indeed in all discussion about policy — the discussion, no less, of how we should together arbi-

trate our lives. We face a barrage of words and terms that claim to represent "reality" in the international world. The terms of foreign affairs are a specialised language within a language, and thus, a subset of a subset of actual experience. Exacerbating the problem, "statesmen", academics and commentators almost daily invent new terms to attempt to describe what is going on. For example, *asymmetric warfare* is a term used, usually though not always, to describe a fight between unequally-equipped combatants, though confusingly it was also recently used by US officials to describe the suicides of a group of Guantanamo detainees, implying perhaps that these were an act of war.

Globalisation is a word bandied around with such abandon (including by me) that all but the vaguest sense of its true meaning has been lost. Coined by the Harvard professor Theodore Leavitt in 1983, the term as invented meant that new technologies had "proletarianised" (Leavitt's own jargon, common at the time but now barely used) communication, transportation and travel, creating worldwide markets for standardised consumer products at lower prices. This careful description has not prevented the word being applied to phenomena as varied as the homogenisation of culture, the loss of native languages or the liberalisation of capital markets. To add to our distress, we must contend with the deconstructionist critique that words carry an unacknowledged political freight and themselves perform a political purpose.

Metaphors ("*ping-pong diplomacy*", "*the axis of evil*") are conjured up to give an organising pattern to matters. In theory, they are supposed to help explain what is going on, but in practice are often meant to shape responses to policy: the *war on terror* is the most notorious example of this phenomenon.[3]

The decision-making of international affairs is often presented as a calculus, that economic interest X plus security need Y equals policy Z (though as I discuss elsewhere such a representation implies a clarity and deliberative rigour that rarely exists in the rush of modern diplomacy). This presents policymaking as essentially rational, based on quantifiable and verifiable facts. Of course, as many honest politicians and diplomats would confess, it is no such thing. For the business of foreign affairs is above all about ordering the collective life of that most complex and immeasurable of beings: the human. Good politicians and good diplomats all employ a hefty dose of personal psychology and human intuition in their otherwise rational analyses (President George Bush for instance has admitted that he watches body language closely).[4] Perhaps we need to confess this more openly.

Some innovations would help the way foreign policy is conventionally discussed and arbitrated now. First, we need constantly to interrogate the terms we use to check their correspondence with reality. It might be better if we tried using simpler terms that everyone can understand; to try, as Wittgenstein urged, to see things as they are. The arms race of neologisms to describe our situation must stop. So perhaps instead of talking about *asymmetric warfare*, we should talk about conflict between grossly unequal parties; instead of *globalisation*, we should talk about the growth in international trade, or the liberalisation of national capital markets, or global income inequality or the homogenisation of national cultures, whichever it is that we mean; and instead of the *post-modern world order*, we should talk about the way the world is organised in the early twenty-first century. Simple language is needed to get to grips with a complicated world.

There are methods to help us understand and arbitrate the non-empirical. The Oxford Research Group, through its Oxford Process, has developed techniques to try to get at the underlying assumptions and emotions at play in political, and in particular conflict, situations. They have realised that there are often deeply embedded philosophical assumptions at work in a political position — about how the world should be organised and how people should behave. Such unquantifiable elements often underpin deep-seated conflict and are yet not addressed — or given weight — in conventional analyses employing the accepted terminology of diplomacy. In organising dialogue sessions between antagonists, the Oxford Group have found that even simple things like providing good food and musical entertainment can contribute substantially to beneficial outcomes. Though seemingly obvious, such aspects are given very little attention in the formal, anti-emotional, masculine-dominated world of traditional diplomacy.

To get to grips with the immeasurable, let alone the indescribable, is more difficult. The language of international affairs is limited; all language, all terms are limited. What lies beyond contains phenomena and components of human existence that are measureless in their importance. This observation sounds, for an atheist like me, uncomfortably close to a declaration of the significance of religion. But at a minimum we should acknowledge the importance of the metaphysical. This is the realm of the artist, the writer, the musician, the moral philosopher, and even the imam, the rabbi or the priest. If art informs us about the nature of ourselves as individuals, why should it not also help us understand our world internationally?[5] The semiotician can help interpret the signs which are not ar-

ticulated by conventional language. In all of this, we should cultivate an eclecticism of source and information.

We need help to navigate this territory beyond the scientific and the rational. For in this province lie questions that no amount of economic theory, models of "statecraft" or quantitative analysis can answer. These include the moral questions about what is the right thing to do and, most fundamentally, how we should live. In a science-obsessed age, we have become used to turning to science, or pseudo-science, for answers, but it is perhaps time to acknowledge the limits of those answers and realise that we need to develop new ways of engaging with and arbitrating the irrational in ourselves.

———————

This, I suspect, was the missing something in the Security Council: the difference between description and reality, the indefinable component of human experience. I cannot be sure, and I cannot prove it. But that there is a gap between talking about, say, genocide in Eastern Congo, and experiencing that horror, is unarguable. That disparity may account for the choice of indifference over action. In my work on Iraq (chapter 3), it without doubt contributed to the crudeness (and cruelty) of sanctions policy. The real experience — and suffering — of the Iraqi people were the absent truths at our negotiating table.

The ambassadors of the Security Council have in recent years made some attempt to bridge the gap by travelling to the trouble spots they are dealing with. But even this commendable effort is limited by the inevitable brevity of the visits and the diplomatic version of Heisenberg's problem whereby the object of observation is

altered by the act of observation. I have no first-hand experience of this but often, I gather, when the ambassadors travel to a region, local interlocutors put down their guns and agree to talk, only to resume fighting as soon as the diplomats have left.

We have no Counsellor Troi to sense the immeasurable. But we do have means to interpret the ineffable of human experience. Every political leader who has effected fundamental change, from Gandhi to Mandela, has given heed to this moral force. Even if we cannot quantify, we can account for — or at a minimum acknowledge — this undeniable constituent of our existence. Failure to do so, Wittgenstein believed, could lead humanity to disaster.

9

THE NEGOTIATION (2)

UN Security Council, New York 1999

In December 1998, the US and UK bombed Iraq in Operation Desert Fox, in retaliation for Iraq's failure to cooperate with the weapons inspectors during a test period earlier that year. It was not until 17 December the following year that the Security Council was able to decide a renewed — but not united — approach to Iraq, on both central issues of sanctions and weapons inspections. That year encompassed some of the hardest work of my life. The product — resolution 1284 — adopted by 11 positive votes, with none against and four abstentions, was one of the longest and most complex UN resolutions ever.

In January the following year, while still at the UK mission, I wrote an article to commit the negotiation to the record. I did so with publication in mind so I utilised the sort of language that I thought was required: the conventional discourse of states and their interests. And this is what I wrote:[1]

As 1999 began, we knew that we had a tough job ahead to rebuild a Council position on Iraq. At that point, we set ourselves three overlapping objectives. The first was to avoid a position where we would have to veto a sanctions-lifting resolution (a step which was in no way justified given Iraq's record of non-compliance). The second was to build up a cushion of support for our position in the Council, thus preventing others from building up support for sanctions-lift. The third was to pass a new resolution, which would clearly re-establish a Council position and reaffirm its commitment to its past resolutions and the necessity of Iraqi compliance. We always judged the third objective to be the most difficult, if not impossible, given the vituperative opposition from Russia and China in particular, but in the end we achieved all three.

As the Council discussed Iraq through January, it became clear that most Council members wanted a fresh approach. Common ground among us was that much more should be done to address the suffering of the Iraqi people, but also that Iraq should comply with its obligations under the resolutions, particularly those relating to disarmament. It was also clear that many members wanted a thorough consideration of the many and complex issues involved, particularly the arcane questions of Iraqi WMD programmes and the intricate and sometimes opaque operation of the oil-for-food programme, a UN-administered scheme whereby Iraq could sell oil in return for humanitarian supplies.

The upshot was the creation of three panels, all chaired by the then Brazilian Ambassador Celso Amorim, addressing disarmament, humanitarian issues and the continuing question of Kuwaiti missing persons and property (for whom Iraq had consistently failed to account). The panels provided a breathing space for the Council to reexamine the issues at stake, and, frankly, to cool down after the bitter arguments of 1998. The reports the panels produced provided the building blocks for a new Council approach.

As soon as the panels reported in March 1999, it was clear that the mood in the Council was to take forward the work of the panels and put the bulk of their recommendations into action. The Council needed to design a comprehensive way forward, one that set out a route map to deal with Iraq's obligations to dispose of and account for its WMD, but also one that addressed the humanitarian needs of the Iraqi people.

To do this, the UK drafted a new comprehensive draft resolution, which took forward the panel recommendations in the three main areas (disarmament, humanitarian and Kuwaiti issues). Our draft provided for the creation of a new disarmament body to take over the work of UNSCOM. It also took forward a series of measures to improve the resources available to, and the operation of, the oil-for-food programme, principally by removing the ceiling limiting Iraqi oil sales but also by simplifying the procedures for the import of goods into Iraq and allowing the UN to spend money locally to revive the economy. On the third set of issues, the draft resolution took up the panel recommendation for the appointment of a new UN Special Coordinator to press for Iraqi compliance with its obligations to account for the missing Kuwaiti persons and property.

But in addition to these provisions, the resolution provided a new stepping stone on the path to the lifting of sanctions. The draft's most important provision was to allow for the suspension (rather than the full lifting) of sanctions if Iraq fulfilled a list of key disarmament tasks, which would be identified by the disarmament commission. This offered a new, interim step to Iraq, short of the full lift-for-full compliance equation of the earlier resolutions. Instead of "light at the end of the tunnel", there was also "light in the middle of the tunnel". This was a crucial innovation in gathering support for the resolution.

The Struggle for the "Middle Ground"

Thus began the first phase of our campaign. Led by Ambassador Sir Jeremy Greenstock, we embarked on a long and detailed lobbying exercise, focused primarily on the non-permanent members whom we called the "middle ground" of the Council: those Council members who supported neither the immediate lifting of sanctions, nor the perpetuation of the "ancien regime". The Netherlands was the first to cosponsor our resolution, and the draft resolution thus became known as the "Anglo-Dutch" draft. The Dutch were to provide robust and energetic support throughout our campaign.

Others took longer to convince, and a gruelling and lengthy process of addressing each member's concerns one by one took place. Countries like Canada and Brazil had, like us, thought long and hard about the Iraq problem. They had strong views about particular issues: for example the Canadians believed that there should be provision, if Iraq was cooperating with the UN, for foreign oil companies to be allowed back into Iraq to invest in the country's decaying oil infrastructure, thus to allow more revenues to be produced for the humanitarian programme. Brazil, having chaired the panels, had a number of concerns, in particular on the operation of the humanitarian programme. They, and others, were insistent that if suspension of sanctions took place, it should cover imports into Iraq as well as exports from Iraq. Among the non-permanents, there was also widespread resistance to the Anglo-Dutch draft resolution's provision (taken from the panel recommendations) that the UN's compensation fund, set up after the Gulf War to compensate those who had suffered losses caused by the invasion, should be raided for funds to supplement the humanitarian programme in Iraq. Another factor was perhaps the desire of some non-permanents, particularly those with a well-developed sense of the injustice of the permanent/non-permanent division in the Council, not to be too easily bidden in this, the

most tendentious of Council issues. But after detailed discussion, backed up by the usual political lobbying by embassies in capitals, particularly by the US, and by phone-calls between foreign ministers, we slowly built up the list of co-sponsors. By August we had a list of nine co-sponsors, thus achieving the first and second of our objectives.

Close coordination with the US during this phase was crucial, as it was throughout. The presentation of our draft resolution was discussed in detail with the administration in Washington. Both our officials in London and New York, on frequent visits and phonecalls to Washington, and our embassy in Washington, kept in constant contact with all the key actors in the administration, not all of whom were easily convinced of the merits of our approach. Some were undoubtedly more ready to discard the Council approach, frustrated by those in the Council who seemed far too keen to appease the Iraqis, and preferred instead a more unilateral approach to military containment.

We argued that the British and American common interest in limiting the Iraqi threat was best achieved by restoring international support in the Council. A new Council resolution was the best way to get a robust inspection mechanism back into Iraq and to consolidate support for the international effort to secure Iraqi compliance with its obligations.

An additional argument was the fear that the absence of a new resolution would encourage others to come forward with proposals to lift sanctions, which we would have to resist as utterly unjustified. In the end these arguments, which were shared by the bulk of administration officials, particularly in the State Department, won through. The US ultimately decided, like us, that a multilateral approach to dealing with Iraq was better than going it alone. Their support was essential. A simple reality of today's Security Council is that no resolution will prosper without it.

While we were engaged in our campaign for support, others were waging their own campaigns. The French, Russians and Chinese presented alternative draft resolutions in a number of different permutations (a tripartite working paper, a French working paper and a Russian/Chinese working paper were the main proposals). The difference between their and our proposals is encapsulated in the distinction, seemingly arcane but nonetheless important, between compliance and cooperation. The Russian, Chinese and French proposals offered Iraq the suspension and lifting of sanctions in return merely for cooperation *with the new disarmament mechanism (the original Russian draft offered suspension in return for Iraq simply allowing the inspectors back into Iraq). We insisted on actual compliance with Iraq's obligations, i.e. the material revelation of information about WMD programmes or matériel of those programmes. It was never clear what cooperation would mean if there was no compliance. [US diplomat] Thomas Pickering at one point later in the negotiations compared it to offering the new UNSCOM tea and biscuits.*

These countries were as vigorous as we were in arguing the merits of their approach, claiming above all that theirs was the only "realistic" way forward in the light of Iraq's antipathy to any further arms inspections and its statements that it would only cooperate if offered the immediate lifting of sanctions. But only Malaysia declared full sympathy with the alternative approach. Other Council members were more ready to agree with us that the Council's credibility would be undermined if we discarded our own conditions for sanctions relief, simply because Iraq had failed to meet theirs.

The P5 Process

By the summer therefore, we had a majority of Council members supporting our resolution, but it was clear that divisions in the P5 were entrenched. We

realised that we would need a new approach to attempt to win consensus in the Council, or failing that, adoption of the resolution with the largest possible majority (and, by implication, no vetoes). No one wanted the impasse to last any longer, or wanted Council divisions to become set in stone. But equally the positions in the P5, between the US and UK on the one hand, and Russia, China and France on the other, were still far apart.

Diplomatic activity traditionally is a little quieter in the summer months. That August, we sat down in London and worked out a strategy to try to get the P5 together. We decided to adopt a French suggestion of working on "floating elements" of a resolution, rather than continuing to flog our national text, in order to get round national sensitivities over ownership of the text. (One should never underestimate the attachment a country forms to its own text, much as individuals do.) We would divide the resolution into its main components, covering disarmament, humanitarian and Kuwaiti issues. We would then initiate discussion of each of these elements separately, on the basis that nothing was agreed until everything was agreed. Each part of the discussion would begin on a general basis: we would work on concepts, before trying to work up detailed language for a resolution.

We initiated this phase of our campaign with a P5 meeting of Political Directors in London in September. Discussion went well, though there were still large differences. There was a clear willingness at least to try to overcome our differences. After this meeting, contacts continued by telephone and via bilateral meetings, in particular between France, the UK and the US.

The first week of the General Assembly in New York (so-called ministerial week) is always an intense few days of diplomatic activity. We decided to take advantage of the week's hothouse atmosphere and the presence of everyone's senior officials and foreign ministers, to try for a breakthrough. Tactically, we chose to abandon temporarily our "floating elements" approach, and attempted instead to win agreement to a more general P5 statement of common

principles in our approach to Iraq (a technique copied from the Kosovo G8 statement negotiation, where it had proved effective). The technique failed. A week's intensive discussion among senior officials produced no agreement on a common statement.

Looking back, I am not sure the statement would have helped us agree a resolution in any case. While it was difficult enough to agree common principles on handling Iraq, the real nub of our argument lay in the detailed language of the resolution regarding the conditions for the suspension of sanctions, and other issues such as the composition of the new disarmament body. This was to become more apparent later in the process. Nonetheless, the ministerial week discussions allowed the arguments to be fully aired, and some closer understanding of each others' positions to be achieved. Perhaps above all, the ministerial week discussions helped to dispel some of the suspicion of US and UK motives that had grown up, particularly after Operation Desert Fox, that we were seeking to pass a resolution simply as a pretext for the further use of force (since Iraq was likely, initially at least, to reject it). But we had hoped that the week's discussions would result in a helpful boost to our efforts on the resolution, through a substantive common statement from the P5 Foreign Ministers who met at the end of the week. This did not happen.

Instead, we pressed on with P5 meetings in New York. Meanwhile, contacts also continued in parallel, principally between London, Paris and Washington. In the course of these trilateral discussions, conducted at senior official level, we were able tentatively to agree a form of words for the most tendentious element of the resolution, namely the conditions for the suspension and lifting of sanctions, which had become known as "the trigger". In the P5 forum, the principal bones of contention were the composition of the new disarmament body (where Russia wanted all residue of UNSCOM excised) and the trigger. It became clear that this latter issue was the only

one that really mattered: if we could get agreement to that, then we could get agreement to everything else.

We were able, after extensive discussion, to find common ground on the humanitarian provisions of the resolution (with one or two small points, such as provision for Umra pilgrimage flights, still outstanding) and, to a large extent, on the establishment and composition of the new disarmament body, to be known as UNMOVIC (an acronym resulting from my tortured attempt to incorporate the key initials of Monitoring, Verification, Inspection and Commission.).[2]

On the disarmament body, Russia's demands hardened as discussions went on, including the demand that no UNSCOM staff should be allowed to serve in the new body and that all references to "full" cooperation by Iraq should be removed, as these were "provocative" and could be used as a pretext for military action if Iraq failed to provide full cooperation. But despite this, the final language that resulted was broadly acceptable to all of us: UK and US concerns were satisfied that the new body should enjoy the full rights of access to Iraqi installations (immediate access, anywhere, anytime) and that it should be staffed by serious disarmament experts, including those who had worked for UNSCOM.

But it was the trigger that took up most of our time, in meeting after meeting, variously in our separate missions, in dingy rooms in the UN building, and finally in the well-provisioned chambers of the US Mission as the negotiations drew to their close. At the beginning of the P5 process, we had decided that we should not attempt to agree how suspension would take place i.e. what controls would remain on Iraq to prevent WMD rearmament after the suspension of sanctions. This would unnecessarily burden the already-tortuous discussions with an issue that we did not need to resolve until after the resolution had passed. Fortunately, the other P5 quickly agreed to this: France in particular realised early on that trying to resolve this issue would

make negotiations more difficult rather than easier. Instead discussion focussed on <u>when</u> and under what conditions sanctions should be suspended.

The End-Game

As the autumn months slipped by, we knew discussion could not last indefinitely. The pressure was on us, particularly from the region, to get a result. With the membership of the Council changing at the end of the year, when four of our cosponsors would leave the Council, time was running out. We stepped up the pace of meetings, and encouraged attendance from capitals to reduce the scope for delay.

As discussion headed into its final weeks, it became clear that the ambiguity inherent in the trigger language we, the French and Americans had worked out together, was becoming more a hindrance than a help. This text in complex language essentially said that sanctions suspension would be decided by the Council after a report by the new Executive Chairman of UNMOVIC that Iraq had cooperated for 120 days and that this report would also cover progress made by Iraq in fulfilling the key disarmament tasks (even this description is a simplification of what the resolution contains). Russia, in the form of its vigorous and tenacious Permanent Representative, teased away at this language, demanding to know what precisely was meant by progress and insisting that all ambiguity be removed. We argued that whether the progress was sufficient to trigger the suspension of sanctions was something only the Council could judge at the time. In other words, the decision should be deferred. We, the French and the Americans realised that such ambiguity was the only way we could conceivably bridge our differences.

It emerged that behind this textual difference lay deeper political differences that perhaps could never have been resolved by negotiation on the text. As the negotiations reached their climax, the Russians revealed that they

were working only for a resolution on which Russia could abstain. They were not aiming to vote for the resolution. China echoed this position. France in the end confirmed that it too would only abstain if the resolution could not be unanimously supported, despite the extensive work we had done together on the text. Naturally, we were disappointed to hear this news, particularly from the French.

I do not know why these countries decided to abstain. No doubt, like all of us, they in the end made a calculation of their overall interests, including their relationship with Iraq. The Iraqi Prime Minister visited Moscow in early December and argued that Russia should veto the resolution. The Russians may have concluded that abstention provided them with a good balance: it would avoid unnecessarily irritating the Iraqis (with whom they have well-known common interests, in terms of debt owed and oil contracts in the offing) but also minimise damage to relations with the West, which would undoubtedly have been undermined by a Russian veto (the Chechnya campaign had recently begun). As for the French, they argued to us that a non-unanimous resolution would be diminished in force, and the Iraqis would be unlikely to comply — in its way a self-fulfilling argument.

By the second week of December, it was clear to all concerned that further negotiation would achieve little. There seemed no further point in massaging the trigger language when only a Russian abstention was on offer in any case. The precision the Russians were demanding would have made the conditions for suspension too lenient, reducing to an unacceptable degree the obligations on Iraq and the real leverage on the Iraqi government to cooperate. In any case, the Russian declaration of intent to abstain naturally reduced our and the Americans' willingness to consider further concessions. The French, perhaps the most discomfited by the prospective outcome before them, were the last to accept this reality and insisted on further attempts to bridge the gaps, but these in the end proved futile.

When we finally took the resolution to the vote on 17 December, we knew that all efforts to reach consensus had been exhausted. It was therefore the best possible outcome we could have achieved in the circumstances. The negotiations had lasted perhaps ten months (depending on where you judge that they began); in any case they lasted far longer than we had anticipated. Exhausting though the effort was, the sheer duration of the talks demonstrated to everyone that every attempt had been made to obtain agreement. I doubt if anyone will be keen to repeat our effort for a new comprehensive resolution for some time yet.

At the adoption, every Council member, including those who abstained (Malaysia joined China, Russia and France), stated that the new resolution represented a new, and indeed the only, way forward for the UN's relationship with Iraq. As I write in January 2000, work on implementation of the resolution has begun, as have the efforts to persuade the Iraqis to comply (the Russians, Chinese, French and Malaysians have all called on Iraq to comply with SCR 1284). This may prove a long task. But Iraq must in the end heed the reality that compliance with the resolution is the only way out of sanctions and back to a normal relationship with the rest of the world.

I was not allowed to send the article for publication. The British embassies in Paris and Washington both opined that its publication might risk offending their hosts.

Looking back, the self-confident, if not triumphalist, tone of the piece is as striking as its employment of a very particular form of writing to describe the events in which I had participated. Instead of writing, for example, what the "Russian ambassador said", I wrote what "Russia wanted". Note too the repeated and uncon-

scious use of the "we" word to describe UK policy. But what is more striking now is that what I wrote is not how I remember what actually took place.

For instance, I wrote that the "middle ground" countries like Brazil and Canada all had particular national concerns about what should go into the resolution. But when I remember now, I realise that this was not what I actually observed. For when the ambassador and I talked to the members of these delegations, as we did many times, one rather startling truth was evident, and that was that these supposedly "national concerns" were not "national" concerns at all.

Since the negotiation had become framed as a great big negotiation about what the Council should "do" about Iraq, many of the "experts", myself included, had developed a lot of whizz-bang ideas about how to untangle the Gordian knot. This was after all our job, or as we chose to see it. The Canadian, Brazilian and Slovene "experts" (my opposite numbers) were no different, and had all taken it upon themselves to develop particular hobby-horses. The Canadian expert had become obsessed with the oil issue, and in particular about something called Production Sharing Agreements; the Brazilian with various arcane aspects of the humanitarian issue. These personal interests became transformed into national concerns.

For what we found when we lobbied their ambassadors was that they rarely understood the supposedly national concerns on which their experts had briefed them. For instance, I prepared my ambassador for a detailed, technical discussion of the oil investment issue with the Canadian ambassador, only to discover that the Canadian had the flimsiest grasp of what was allegedly a serious national concern. This did not prevent the latter from insisting the provision he wanted be included in the resolution. When our High Commission

(as embassies in the British Commonwealth are known) in Ottawa talked to "Ottawa", i.e. the Canadian Foreign Ministry, they told our diplomats that the concerns were all entirely generated by the expert in New York.

If the delegations became particularly obdurate, we would ask London to send in our embassies in the countries concerned to find out what the foreign ministries thought about their "national concerns". Without exception, we found that Brasilia, Ottawa or whichever capital were either completely unaware of what their delegations were doing in their name or that, if they were not unaware, they took no interest whatsoever in the content of the issue at stake. Sometimes the ambassadors chose to adopt their experts' concerns as their own and thus of their country, sometimes they did not. It was, it seemed to me, entirely arbitrary and in any case it didn't really matter.

What mattered in winning over the "middle ground" was not the deliberation over the actual content of the resolution — but rather the political arm-twisting that went on to get the non-permanents to see matters "our" way. It was clear to those countries, and if it wasn't clear it was made clear to them that in the final analysis they would of course have to end up supporting us, or rather the US. There was no way that, put to a vote, the Canadians, Slovenes or Brazilians would vote against us. This message was usually conveyed in private telephone calls between foreign ministers or, in the case of Slovenia, during a state visit by the US President. It was merely a question of how long it took for them to get the message. You will notice that this version of events makes no appearance in my so-called "insider's account of the negotiation", as I had titled my article.

Reading the resolution now,[3] I am appalled by its ludicrous complexity. The "trigger" section (section D) is almost unintelligible: even at the time of its adoption, I suspect that only a very few people — and I was one of them — could have explained what it actually *meant*. Read, if you can bear, just one of the paragraphs setting out the conditions for the trigger:

```
33. Expresses its intention, upon receipt
of reports from the Executive Chairman
of UNMOVIC and from the Director General
of the IAEA that Iraq has cooperated in
all respects with UNMOVIC and the IAEA in
particular in fulfilling the work programmes
in all the aspects referred to in paragraph
7 above, for a period of 120 days after the
date on which the Council is in receipt of
reports from both UNMOVIC and the IAEA that
the reinforced system of ongoing monitoring
and verification is fully operational, to
suspend with the fundamental objective of
improving the humanitarian situation in
Iraq and securing the implementation of
the Council's resolutions, for a period
of 120 days renewable by the Council, and
subject to the elaboration of effective
financial and other operational measures to
ensure that Iraq does not acquire prohibited
items, prohibitions against the import of
commodities and products originating in Iraq,
and prohibitions against the sale, supply
and delivery to Iraq of civilian commodities
and products other than those referred to
in paragraph 24 of resolution 687 (1991) or
those to which the mechanism established
by resolution 1051 (1996) applies;
```

This complexity was a function of the political divisions underlying the text. We could not agree, hence we sought resolution in ambiguities. This approach was to have its own price later.

Sandy Berger, then US National Security Adviser, once described the text of the resolution as "talmudic" in its complexity and "humongous" in its difficulty. Because of this complexity, and despite the gravity of the issue, the negotiations were conducted to a very large extent by diplomats. There was only occasional involvement by senior politicians at crucial moments. Usually when this happened, the ministers would be quite unable to get to grips with the tangled syntax and esoteric symbolisms of the words (such as the difference between cooperation and compliance). This was understandable given the short time ministers invariably had to prepare for such contacts. Their interventions were therefore of little help, except for the arm-twisting that went on to get the non-permanents on-board (arm-twisting didn't work with the P5).

The views and prejudices of the sometimes quite junior diplomats therefore mattered more than I had suspected. Some contributed a great deal to the resolution and our effort to reach agreement (including among those who later abstained). Some did not. One member of a P5 delegation was especially destructive. After a long day's negotiation, I would return to my Mission to write the telegram for London recording what had happened. The next morning I would return to the office to see the reports from our embassies in the other P5 capitals on their thoughts on the state of play of the negotiations. The report from his capital retailed a version of the previous day's discussion which I could not recognise. In every case, the worst possible interpretation had been placed upon what we and, above all, the Americans were saying. This was very much to

the detriment of our aim of agreement and indeed I am convinced it contributed to his country's decision to abstain. But it would be wrong to single out one diplomat for putting his own personal interpretation on what was going on, because, to greater and lesser degrees, that was what we were all doing.

One of the things you realise when participating in a process like this is how personal it is. We would negotiate for hours in small, uncomfortable little rooms (often the "P5 room" off the corridor leading to the Security Council). What went on in there was reduced by me, and my colleagues in other missions, into neat, tidy summary records which were transmitted back to our capitals ("Russia proposed x; US conceded y"). It was for me, with the endorsement of my ambassador who checked what I wrote, to decide what was important and what was not and how to report it. If we felt we needed more negotiating room from London, we would exaggerate the extent of opposition on that point. If we didn't like our instructions from London on another point, we would emphasise our opponents' arguments against it. This much I think any negotiator under the control of a distant authority would understand.

But there was something more too. Particularly during discussion of the trigger, which had become a very intimate P5 affair, conducted largely by the ambassadors with the experts at their side, there were things going on which did not fit into the conventional reports we were required to write home. I remember one particular afternoon during a P5 meeting in the US mission when agreement seemed within our grasp. It rested partly on the interpretation of a word but partly on something much more intangible, describable only by words like goodwill and trust. When the history of this episode will be written, it will no doubt adopt an analysis based solely upon the

interaction of interests. But how the negotiators interpreted those interests and how they chose to report our expression of our positions involved an altogether more personal aspect.

Sitting in the upstairs conference room of the US mission on First Avenue, the UN complex across the street, I sometimes had the feeling that agreement was hanging in the air above the darkly veneered conference table like some hovering phantom. If we all reached out for it at once it would become real; instead we were swiping at it one by one, failing to make the connection.

What was this about? A word that never appeared in my telegrams reporting the talks, which, looking back, I think should have done. Trust. Intangible and immeasurable, it was a component that would, if extant, have comprised the missing piece in our jigsaw puzzle. The Russians, who were by some way the most tenacious in their opposition to and criticism of our approach, simply did not trust that our intentions were not once more to find a pretext to attack Iraq. Underlying that distrust may have lain an interest in preserving the political status quo in Iraq which was, theoretically, beneficial to Russia's economic interests, but had the distrust been erased then we would have known more clearly that the interests were the motor.

It is always easy to attribute to one's opponents the base and selfish motives of economic interest. This is how the British and American press routinely described French and Russian motives in their analyses of why those countries refused to support the US military campaign in 2003. Meanwhile, to ourselves, we routinely attribute "higher" motives of security, democracy, freedom, when of course the material motives are, with only a few exceptions, also at play.

But I have often felt, looking from inside the box of policy-making, that it is too simplistic to assign motives in this way.

The 2003 war is discussed in chapter 4, but I do not share the view of those who think the war was "about" oil, any more than I think French and Russian opposition (or indeed German or anyone else's) opposition was "about" their economic interest in the existing regime. From my experience, and I have talked to a number of senior diplomats and foreign policy-makers who share this view, only very rarely do decision-makers set down a list of their motives, objectives and "interests". More generally, this is an unordered and iterative process where a paradigmatic view of a situation is built up and then continually reinforced until, in a process similar to the shifts in scientific views described by Thomas Kuhn,[4] something dramatic happens that forces that view to change.[5] Those involved in formulating and expounding the view accumulate a series of facts to justify their interpretation. I suspect that the Russians do this just as much as we do.

Though their position may also have been "about" economic interests, even based upon those interests, the Russians genuinely believed that the US had no intention ever to lift sanctions regardless of Iraqi performance on disarmament. There was much evidence to support this view. President Clinton had said so publicly. The US insistence, during the inspection process, that only absolute and complete fulfilment of every last stipulated obligation of the resolutions would lead to movement on sanctions — *what* movement they invariably refused to specify — reinforced the impression. In 1998 the IAEA had reported that Iraq had met its obligations to disarm itself verifiably of its nuclear weapons-making capability, barring two minor issues. In the Security Council both the US and we refused

to agree a statement giving public acknowledgement of this achievement, which was undoubted progress by the Iraqis. This instance in particular was often mentioned to me by the Iraqis, French and Russians as a case of bad faith: if the Iraqis were making progress we should at a minimum say so and pay public heed. But we did not — the US delegation told us that in domestic political terms the Administration could not make any suggestion that Saddam was doing as he was supposed to.

There was a personal aspect too. The Russian ambassador felt that he had been lied to, both by the US and UK and by Richard Butler, the head of UNSCOM. Before Desert Fox took place, we had managed to squeeze out of the Council a resolution yet again demanding that Iraq give UNSCOM full cooperation. During the negotiation, Ambassador Sergei Lavrov specifically asked us, in the Council Chamber, whether we regarded the language of the resolution as authorising the use of military force in the event of Iraqi non-cooperation. We responded that it did not. And yet, when Desert Fox arrived, we did indeed use this resolution as part of our legal justification for the use of force (a similar trick was pulled before the 2003 war). Lavrov was also obsessed by what he claimed was Butler's deliberate deceit in telling the Russians in Moscow that Iraq was cooperating, shortly before returning to New York to issue his report stating that Iraq had not in fact cooperated.

During the P5 negotiation there was a particular moment that stands out highlighted in my memory (again, unmentioned in my article). The Russian ambassador asked the US delegate (that day it was an Assistant Under-Secretary from Washington) straight out about what was *really* the US position on sanctions, specifically, what would Iraq qualify for in terms of sanctions lift if it met the

conditions set out in resolution 687? (The paragraphs in this resolution established what Iraq must do in terms of disarming itself of its WMD and missiles in order for sanctions to be *lifted,* which means that sanctions are irrevocably terminated, rather than *suspended,* which means what it says, i.e. that sanctions are suspended but could later be reimposed.) The US official looked discomfited and stared around him, clearly unprepared for so direct a question. After an uncomfortable and telling pause, "Suspension, at a minimum" was his reply and he looked disquieted offering even this generous an interpretation of US policy, something which no member of the Administration would bring himself to say publicly, for fear of seeming "soft" on Saddam.

This statement — that the US would only *suspend* sanctions if Iraq met the conditions for *lift* — seems relatively innocuous but, to the *cognoscenti*, it was highly loaded. It sent a shock through the French and Russian delegations. The experts feverishly scribbled down the quotation, word for word. I knew immediately that "we" had scored a major own-goal. I am sure that the telegrams transmitted back to Paris and Moscow that evening highlighted this very point in triplicate. Perhaps it was brought to the special attention of Putin and Chirac when, a few weeks later, they were making their final decisions on how to vote. The US had admitted, in all candour and in a private negotiating chamber, that even if Iraq met the conditions for *lift,* it would only agree to the *suspension* of sanctions. For the French and Russians, this was proof positive that the US was acting in bad faith: while demanding the fullest possible compliance from Iraq down to the last letter of the resolutions, it was not prepared to keep its side of the bargain by lifting sanctions, even if Iraq met those conditions.

That year of negotiation was partly about finding a point at which the differing views of the Iraq issue, above all among the P5, could find convergence. Our lengthy discussions were about texts and words, and as they were reported, were a process of finding forms of those words, terms and compromises to produce that meeting point. If a historian were to examine the documentary record (I alone must have written hundreds of detailed telegrams about this one negotiation), that is what he or she would see. This is the narrative form that my article, quoted above, would take. The press, denied access to our little chamber, reported this anodyne version of events, fed to them by press officers highly fluent in the discourse.

But it was also about trust among small groups of people (all men). In each country, only a small number of people were involved in deciding what each country wanted. We had all been deeply, perhaps too deeply, immersed in this complex and tortured subject. Trust was the evanescent phantom that escaped us. And that moment, when the US official replied to the Russian's question, was the moment when I realised that it had evaded us for good.

10

INDEPENDENT DIPLOMAT, OR THE
OTHER SIDE OF THE TABLE

"…The wise man belongs to all countries, for the home of a great soul is
the whole world."

Democritus, quoted in Karl Popper, *The Open Society and its Enemies*

Hargeisa, Somaliland

We are driving along the long road from Berbera on the
Red Sea coast, back to Hargeisa, the dusty capital of Somaliland. I am with Edna Adan, the 69-year old foreign minister
of Somaliland, a government driver, Magan from the Ministry and
a bodyguard. This has not always been a safe road; a year ago, a
German aid worker was ambushed here and his Somali companion
shot dead. We've spent the day in Berbera to witness and celebrate
a significant moment in Somaliland's development as a state. Fifty
long steel containers, loaded with wiring and machinery for a large
state electricity company, have been delivered by ship at Berbera

to be trucked to Ethiopia, 150 miles inland up this road. This is the first official trade shipment other than food aid since Somaliland was re-established as a state in 1991. A small moment maybe, but a significant one for this diminutive and young country.

Edna Adan is something of a folk heroine in Somaliland. The former wife of one of Somalia's former prime ministers, she has used her retirement savings and her pension (she worked for the UN) to build and run a maternity hospital in Hargeisa. In a poor town, the hospital is a much-loved institution built from a rubbish tip by a much-loved woman. Wherever we go in Somaliland, she is greeted by patients, parents of patients and simply ordinary people, who stop to thank and admire her.

There hasn't been much traffic; in fact the road has been all but deserted for most of our journey. But in front of us a white car is driving in the middle of the road, preventing us from passing. It's an old car and it is spewing a long black cloud of unfiltered exhaust. Although the windows of our four-by-four are closed, the smoke chokes and irritates us. Our driver accelerates and sounds his horn, but still the car in front doesn't give way. Indeed, it seems deliberately to be blocking our path. The Somalilanders in my car exclaim, "What's he doing?", "He's driving dangerously!" We are a little tense, silently aware of what has happened before on this road. But eventually we get past.

A little later, we stop. Minister Edna (as she is known, or, more often, simply Edna) wants to give the biscuits we have brought for our journey to children we pass. They are poor village children. We can see them chasing goats or simply standing, doing nothing but watching our car go by — a rare sight. Somaliland is one of the poorest countries in the world. The large majority of its people

barely subsists. Our car slows when Minister Edna spots a child. But each time we pull over and the driver and guard gesture to the child, they run away. Minister Edna says that she thinks they've been warned by their mothers to keep away from strangers. The children scamper away, sometimes shouting to one another. Laughing, we drive off.

Too late! While we were at the side of the road, the awful white car has overtaken us again and once more we are trapped in its fumes. Revving and beeping, our driver tries to overtake, but again the dirty white car sits in the middle of the road, blocking our way. We can see the car is filled with men. Annoyed and perhaps a little nervous, the Somalilanders grow more agitated. With a frenzy of horn and engine noise, accompanied by much swerving to and fro across the otherwise empty road, our driver manages to get our car alongside.

Our bodyguard leans out of the window as we pass and gestures at the white car to stop. As they pull over, he jumps out carrying his AK-47 rifle at the ready. Minster Edna tries to stop him, but it's too late and he and our driver are quickly making their points emphatically to the occupants of the white car. They're speaking Somali, but even I can understand what they are saying. I feel nervous.

But within about ten seconds, there is laughter and smiles. The driver of the white car, a young man with the pale, slender mien of many Somalis, emerges from the car. Grinning, he mock-salutes the bodyguard who is now mollified and laughing too. The young man comes to the window. Suddenly, he recognises Minister Edna. He is immediately shy and even more repentant for his bad driving. Apologising, he reaches into our car, tenderly grasps Edna's hand and kisses it, and we move on.

I resigned from the British Foreign Office in September 2004. The breaking point finally came when I testified (in secret) to the official inquiry into the use of intelligence on Iraq's WMD (the Butler Inquiry, as it was known). I wrote down all that I thought about the war, including the available alternatives, its illegality and the misrepresentation of what we knew of Iraq's weapons. Once I had written it, I realised at last, after years of agonising, that I could no longer continue to work for the government.

I sent my testimony to the Foreign Secretary and the head of the Foreign Office (the chief civil servant, known as the Permanent Under-Secretary). Neither replied. My career as a formal diplomat of the British state was over. My testimony to the inquiry was only the proximate reason for my resignation. For years, my disillusionment and doubt about diplomacy had been growing.

During my work on the UN Security Council, I had often been struck by a very obvious imbalance — between the diplomatic resources and skills of the powerful countries, and everyone else. As British diplomats, we had considerable advantages. With reams of telegrams and intelligence reports, I was better briefed than most other diplomats present. Our mission was among the largest at the UN, with squads of diplomats covering every issue. In negotiation, our experienced lawyers could ensure that any textual changes were turned to our benefit. We could consult our capital in real-time without fear of interception: unlike many others around the table, our communications were secure. And the UK took pride in drafting more resolutions than anyone else: we would send regular statistics back to London to prove it.

Such advantages are available to a handful of the world's most powerful countries — China, the US, Russia, France, Britain. By no

coincidence is their real (economic and military) power multiplied by this less-recognised but nonetheless forceful diplomatic power.

Meanwhile, everyone else was at a considerable disadvantage. The numerous smaller UN missions struggle to cover the enormous and proliferating agendas of the UN General Assembly, Security Council and specialised committees with just one or two horribly overworked and under-equipped diplomats. (At the World Trade Organisation in Geneva for instance, many poor countries cannot afford to maintain missions, let alone the experts they need to track and influence highly complex trade negotiations.)

Often those with most at stake are not even allowed into the room where their affairs are being discussed. This imbalance of course does not serve those marginalised, but nor, paradoxically, does it serve the powerful. In this complex and interconnected era, agreements that fail to take into account the interests of all concerned parties are not good or sustainable and too often they fall apart. The ultimate effect is a less stable world. If people are ignored, they tend to find ways — sometimes violent — to get heard.

This was the inspiration behind the foundation of Independent Diplomat, a non-profit diplomatic advisory group. I wanted to try to remedy the diplomatic deficit I had witnessed at the Security Council. The idea was to establish a network of experienced practitioners (former diplomats, international lawyers and skilled analysts) whose expertise would be available to help small, inexperienced or under-resourced countries and political groups with their diplomacy — "a diplomatic service for those who need it most".

I began work in the basement of my flat in south London in the autumn of 2004. Independent Diplomat's first contract, signed early the next year, was with the government of Kosovo, to help advise it

during the UN-supervised process that would determine the province's final status. Kosovo, technically still part of Serbia though governed separately by the UN since 1999, was not allowed any diplomatic representation or a foreign ministry, yet it was required to participate in a complex and highly-charged diplomatic process involving many diplomatic actors (to start with, the UN, the EU and the six countries of the Contact Group who dominate south-east European diplomacy, as well, of course, as Serbia itself).

The philosophy of Independent Diplomat is straightforward. We work for our clients. Unlike many other NGOs or international agencies, we are simply at the disposal of the countries and groups that choose to use us. We try to help our clients, through advice and assistance with diplomatic tools, to achieve their international goals. There is only one important condition. All those we help must be democratic and respectful of international law and human rights. No country is perfect in this regard, but the board of Independent Diplomat, which scrutinises all prospective projects we undertake, must be convinced of the general "direction of travel" of our potential clients. On this ground, we have turned down several groups and countries that have approached us. Our hope is that by helping countries and political groups to use the existing international machinery and international law we are helping reinforce peaceful and lawful means of arbitrating international business.

Our work for our clients consists of behind-the-scenes strategic advice as well as practical assistance with things like communications to the UN Security Council,[1] speeches or formal diplomatic presentations. We don't represent our clients diplomatically or lobby for them. I always felt that the sight of a sharp-suited westerner lobbying for a faraway group in the corridors of Washington or New

York was unconvincing: it spoke more of money than integrity. In any case, having been on the receiving end of such lobbying before, I concluded that the people themselves of a country or region were the most convincing advocates of their own cause.

There is a harder edge to why Independent Diplomat needs to exist. For many of our clients, it is predictable that if they are not heard and their views not taken into account, there may be conflict. Most observers of the Balkans would agree that if the final status process (which is underway as I write this) does not conclude in the formation of a new state of Kosovo, there is likely to be renewed war in that corner of south east Europe. In the Western Sahara, the frustrated wishes of the Saharawi people for self-determination could one day break out into renewed violence, though for the moment the Polisario Front very much abjures it. The ceasefire was agreed in 1991, since when there has not been one iota of progress in fulfilling its conditions.

Though our work is practical, there is also a more subtle element to it. We encourage our clients to be confident and assertive in their demands of the world. It is clear already from our work that many countries and political groups do not feel that the institutions of world diplomacy are "theirs". They find these forums intimidating and forbidding. Any scrap of attention they receive there is gratefully accepted, when in fact our clients, like any citizens of the world, should be demanding their rights as equals, not as *demandeurs*. Despite the high-sounding claims of the UN charter or the European Union, the truth is that a great many people feel excluded from these institutions, and perceive that their relationship with them is not of equality but of supplication. It is perhaps

not surprising that they should feel this, for in many cases, like
Kosovo, they are literally excluded.

By coincidence, our first three clients are self-determination
cases. Though in two of those — Kosovo and Somaliland — the
governments are democratic and running affairs in their territories
(the Polisario do not — yet — control the territory they claim),
as non-states they are not given the same status as states in inter-
governmental forums such as the UN. When Independent Diplomat finally managed to find a way for the Kosovo Prime Minister, a
democratically-elected government leader, to attend discussions of
his own country at the UN Security Council, he was not allowed to
speak or sit at the Council table (unlike, for instance, Serbia) and
he was described, humiliatingly, as a member of the UN Mission
in Kosovo delegation, a group of unelected international officials. I
found his treatment by officials and diplomats at the Council rude
and dismissive, and I said this to my colleagues in the Kosovo delegation. They said they were used to it.

As I write in the summer of 2006, Independent Diplomat has
grown to a handful of staff with two offices in London and New
York. We are planning to open offices in Brussels (to cover the EU),
Addis Ababa (the African Union) and other multilateral diplomatic
centres. We are helped by a wide and growing network of advisers
and experts around the world who help us case-by-case with our
projects. We now have two other long-term clients in addition to
Kosovo: the government of Somaliland and the Polisario Front of
the Western Sahara (see chapter 6).

Though I still work in diplomacy, it is very different from my
career in the British foreign service. What I thought would be difficult has proved easier than I expected and what I thought would

be easy has been harder. As a British diplomat I was steeped in the privilege of membership of the closed circle of powerful countries. Leaving that circle, I thought it would be difficult from the outside to work out what was going on inside. I was worried that because I was an "informal" diplomat, the "real" diplomats would not tell me what they were doing. This has not proved to be the case. To my surprise, most diplomats and officials (such as the UN envoys dealing with the Western Sahara or Kosovo) have been open about their work. Indeed, many seem to use Independent Diplomat as a kind of confessional where they tell us what they really think, rather than what their institutions require them to think.

Given the chance, the frustration, cynicism and despair induced by the official discourse of diplomacy can easily spill out. The formal traditions, terms and morals of diplomacy form a kind of strait-jacket that many of the diplomatic world's denizens are eager to escape from. Officials tell me things as Independent Diplomat that they would never confess when I was a British diplomat. Ambassadors tell me of their secret sympathy for the Saharawis, or the necessity of independence for Kosovo, or their frustration with their ministry (or ministers). Unbound by the official line, their true thoughts are revealed. Members of the great institutions of diplomacy — foreign ministries and multilateral bodies — have asked Independent Diplomat to research policies and ideas that they are not permitted to explore in their official work. This is an unexpected stratum of the world of diplomacy that Independent Diplomat has been able to tap into, and use to the benefit of its clients.

But it has been harder than I expected to establish and fund the institution. Independent Diplomat's clients are by definition the poor and marginalised, and cannot afford to pay the fees that would

sustain a commercial agency. So we have been forced to seek funding to support our work. Naively I thought that fundraising would involve emailing a letter to the various foundations and a large cheque would soon follow in response. After a few emails came back with the stock rejections from junior staff members, it became clear that this expectation was false.

In the world of diplomacy, the idea has been warmly greeted. Many diplomats immediately recognise the diplomatic deficit that Independent Diplomat was set up to address. Indeed many ask why such a group has not been established before, such is the glaring need. But in the world of charitable foundations and other funders, it has been harder to convince. For many diplomacy is still a very closed world. Some have asked me to explain what diplomats actually do. In the human rights-oriented culture of many large foundations, there is a scepticism (well-founded in my experience) that diplomats do any good at all. Most seem to regard them and their habits as inherently amoral, driven by the heartless calculus of realpolitik. Why then would the world need an independent diplomat?

As anyone who has tried to set up a charity or non-governmental organisation will tell you, it's a tough business. There seems to be a kind of Darwinian competition at work for new organisations where the foundations wait to see who will remain standing after their first year or so, to test whether their ideas and commitment are truly viable. Though harsh, it cannot be denied that this technique works. Like the senior officials who decide policy in foreign ministries, the decision-makers in the foundations are guarded by legions of gatekeepers whose job, it seems, is to prevent the hordes of begging NGOs stampeding their bank accounts.

It has taken time therefore to win support — and most crucially funding — for the organisation. My first break came from "Unltd", a foundation that supports social entrepreneurs in Britain. I then was fortunate enough to win a fellowship from the Quaker Joseph Rowntree Charitable Trust. Independent Diplomat's first institutional grant came from George Soros's Open Society Institute, appropriately enough, given that Independent Diplomat was designed to address a deficit Karl Popper would have recognised.

The benefits of Independent Diplomat have been many. The slow rediscovery of my own intellectual independence and conscience has been refreshing. I am reminded of how I felt about politics and the world when a student: invigorated, interested and angry. Somehow, being an official diplomat had drained me of one of the things that defined who I was. It had taught me to defend the existing order rather than noticing its injustices and seeking to change them.

More unexpected has been the radical change of view from the other side of the table. Things look very different when you are a Somalilander or a Kosovar. The world does not seem arranged to suit you, rather the contrary. Global institutions can often seem impenetrable and hostile, in sharp contrast to the days when I was one of the countries that ran them. Nor had I realised how much I had to learn from those with whom Independent Diplomat has worked. I have been humbled by the energy and courage of people like Edna Adan of Somaliland. Working with Independent Diplomat has meant that my colleagues and I now spend a lot of time with her, the Kosovo final status delegation or the leaders of the Polisario Front. We have been required to learn how it is to be in their shoes (a process that never ends). In so doing, I have been introduced to values which are less prominent in my own society, whose rep-

resentatives claim to offer its virtues as a model to the rest of the world. How many ministers in Britain run hospitals funded from their own pension? In Kosovo (described recently in the *Financial Times* as a "moral wasteland"), the hospitality and generosity shown to me and other visitors contrasts uncomfortably with the experience of social behaviour in Britain. "We", it seems, have much to learn as well as to teach.

In spite of these compensations, my mental journey from formal diplomat to Independent Diplomat has not been easy. Casting off the identity of a British diplomat was a painful business. I missed my former colleagues and the comforting sense of rightness that the Foreign Office somehow wordlessly encourages in its staff. I missed the intellectual framework of interests and what "we" thought of as the immediate point of reference when confronted by any new political situation. It was a struggle to learn again how to work things out on my own. At first, this was vertiginous and uncomfortable, so deeply rooted was the mental framework instilled in me. I felt lost without it.

More prosaically, I missed telling people I was a British diplomat and the approving nods that usually followed such a statement. I confess that I enjoyed the status that my career involved (though interestingly now that I am no longer a British diplomat, people no longer flatter me and instead tell me what they *really* think about British diplomacy...). The colleagues with whom I joined "the office" in 1989 are now becoming heads of department, some are ambassadors with large residences and official cars. In the early months I thought of this as another enormous phone bill I couldn't pay thumped on my doormat. I missed the comradeship and team spirit — "the office's" virtues.

In parallel to this personal disorientation, I felt a more political fragmentation. When I read the press or travelled, the old sense of order and certainty I had enjoyed as a British diplomat fell away. The forces I saw at work in the world, of economy, belief and human behaviour, seemed less and less under the control of governments and the organs of international cooperation. The world appeared much more complicated and chaotic than it had when depicted in the flow of telegrams and memos which had hitherto comprised the lens through which I saw it. The international meetings, with their grand statements and assumption of control, continued. But now I was no longer part of them, it was not mandatory to believe their claim to be in command of events. Indeed, it seemed clearer and clearer that they were not.

This was disconcerting. As a diplomat but also as an ordinary person, I had been comforted by the belief that the ubiquitous "they" of governments were in control of matters, that if things went wrong, they could put it right. Now I had seen how wrong governments could be, and how poorly they understood the situations they claimed to be arbitrating, I could no longer pretend to be comforted. Like Neo in *The Matrix*, I felt I had taken the red pill and seen the world as it really was, rather than as we wished to believe it: the desert of the real.

On September 11, 2001 I was in New York at the British mission to the UN. Like millions of others, I witnessed the event that triggered the "War on Terror". I experienced the horror and grief on the streets of New York (my apartment was on Union Square where crowds would gather to mourn). That night, I told a friend that governments would seize the chance to reassert themselves.

From the inside, I watched my government adopt the US Administration's naming and framing of their reaction, from using the name "9/11" (no one in New York called it that until Washington did), to the adoption of the metaphor of the "War on Terror". It was clear from the beginning that this nomenclature implied, deliberately, a particular response: militaristic, a-legal. That it also played straight into the hands of Al-Qaeda, who sought and revelled in the status of enemy of the West, seemed not to occur to its originators. This was obvious to all those like me who had worked on the Middle East and watched Al-Qaeda for years. It was equally obvious that any solution to the "terrorist" problem would require at last addressing the noxious and enduring problems of the Middle East — in particular Israel's occupation of the Palestinian territories, the case above all others that drove the sense of injustice and the accusation of the West's "double standards" in its approach to the Muslim world.

Four years later I was in London when suicide bombers, young men from my own country, struck the underground and buses. The invasions of Afghanistan or Iraq had not undermined the appeal — or rather the anger — that drove young men to kill others. Instead, they had strengthened it. Governments — Russia, the US, Britain — continue to use the word "terrorist" and now "Islamic fascist" as a means of closing off discussion of the deeper causes of conflict, ones which they show no intention of addressing, whether in Palestine, Chechnya or anywhere else. Meanwhile, these governments claim that the "terrorists" are attacking our "values" or "freedoms", when even the most cursory reading of the motives of the terrorists shows that it is our governments' policies in the Middle East that provide at least part of the cause of their rage, rather than our "way of life".

All such governments want to pretend, and their populations — like me — want to believe, that they are capable of protecting their people and controlling the affairs of the world. In the disorder of the early twenty-first century, they seem less and less able, just as their rhetoric becomes more and more strident. We seem caught in a spiral, where the more our governments use brutal tactics to defend their claim to protect us, the more they will incite those who wish to attack us. As long as this goes on, we can only expect more violence and disorder.

The cliché of contemporary discussion of international affairs is a cliché for a reason: more and more of our problems are transnational in nature, and do not lend themselves to solution by individual states but only by collective action. Terrorism is one, but so are disease (SARS, bird flu), global warming and migration. To deal with these issues, the traditional calculus of identifying one country's interests, then arbitrating these with other countries, makes little sense. The causes of these problems are complex, and their solutions require detailed, long-term and collective action.

For all the novelty of these global crises, the challenge is still a basic and familiar one: how can we govern the world? How can we design and implement good, effective policy?

Over fifty years ago, Karl Popper pondered this problem and produced in *The Open Society and its Enemies* a vigorous and thorough exposition of why democracy was the only effective system of government. The dilemma we must deal with today is that there is no global democracy. Those designing policy whose impact may be felt worldwide have scant access to those experiencing its effects. It is unarguable therefore that we need ways for those affected by international policy to respond to those who formulate and implement

it, whether in the Security Council in New York, or Washington or Moscow. Independent Diplomat is one small way of tackling that problem. I hope it will grow and expand, for the need is great, as the many governments and political groups that approach us bear witness. But even I would not claim that alone it would be enough.

11

CONCLUSION
THE END OF "DIPLOMACY"?

"Politics is the art of preventing people from taking part in affairs which properly concern them."

Paul Valéry

All politics, said Tip O'Neill, long-time Speaker of the US House of Representatives, is local. He was wrong.

There is not one aspect of our contemporary lives, save our private emotions, which is not in some way affected by what is going on elsewhere in the world. Perhaps even our emotions are not immune, given the omnipresent and insidious effects of our economic, cultural and physical environment. Globalisation has done for the notion of locality what the internet has done for the paper letter. All politics is international.

The spread of global markets and global production has made us familiar with how jobs in south Wales or Pennsylvania are affected by wage levels in the Pearl River Delta. But how is it that a subsidy for cows can affect immigration? (The answer is that agricultural subsidies in Europe and the US reduce export earnings in devel-

oping countries, and thus income and employment levels, thereby increasing pressures for migration, legal or, more often, illegal.) Plans for your retirement can be affected by your employer's need to reduce pensions in order to keep costs as low as its Chinese or Korean competitors (as General Motors has discovered).[1] In the European Union food standards require your morning boiled egg to be of particular colour and shape. Worldwide, the food we eat, as well as the quality of the air we breathe, is more and more a function if not of internationally-imposed rules, then of internationally-propagated norms. Everything is connected.

It's hard now to name one aspect of our contemporary existence that does not have an international aspect. Even things which were once thoroughly local — fashion, celebrity — are more and more international. Benetton or Louis Vuitton are as recognised on the streets of Johannesburg as they are in São Paulo.

Ease of travel and the vast disparity between life in some rich countries and everyone else has created vast flows of migration which are changing societies as fast as any social movement, even revolutions, in their history. Over 200 million people now live outside their country of origin, according to a recent UN survey, up 25% since 1990 (and doubtless accelerating). Global culture not only means that everyone knows Britney Spears or MTV. It also means that street gangs in Sierra Leone (and, in its earlier civil war, its murderous militias) emulate the culture — and the easy violence — of South Central Los Angeles. Our world is in flux.

This observation is now so widely accepted as to be utterly banal. But what is very odd about our globalised world of the twenty-first century is that we still use nineteenth and twentieth-century ways of arbitrating it. The diplomatic machinery and modes of thinking about

international relations have hardly changed at all. "International relations" and "foreign affairs" are treated as separate discourses when
in reality they are thoroughly intrinsic to — and inseparable from
— everything else. Indeed, the separation into a discrete discourse
has created an artificiality of thought both among the practitioners
and those who study them.

At universities, students attend courses on "international relations" where they are taught theories — liberalism, neo-liberalism,
realism — which attempt to give order to this maelstrom. In legislatures, discussion of foreign affairs is sequestered in special committees and debates which few attend, where "specialists" analyse
the doings of Iran, Israel or Venezuela as if they were amoebae in
a Petri dish (invariably essentialising of course). Meanwhile, rarely
bothered by the attentions of those whom they are supposed to be
serving, the diplomats, un-named and mostly un-scrutinised, go
about their business.

As the international aspect of politics becomes more important,
domestic politics has become ever more nugatory and trivial. In the
West, the policy differences between political parties have shrunk
as they converge around liberal-market policies. Denied meaty
policy to argue over, politics focuses on personality (witness Italy's
2006 parliamentary election) and individual credibility in delivering
otherwise almost identical policy. Yet voters feel instinctively that
big stuff is going on, and they're right. Migration, globalisation and
terrorism have combined to create a deep sense of insecurity. These
forces are of course at play all over the world, in China as well as
South Africa. And we all need a politics that is able to come to terms
with them.

At a theoretical level, we are confronted with Karl Popper's deficit. Democracy works at the national level: the electorate provides the feedback to government (through elections and other means), thus enabling government to correct inevitably inaccurate policy (policy is inevitably inaccurate because no government can have perfect knowledge). This feedback system — democracy's greatest virtue — does not function at the international level. Those affected by decisions made in international forums, or those affected in country B by the policies of country A, have no way to inform the decision-makers of the rightness or wrongness of their policies. There is no democracy in international affairs.

There are a number of ways to start to address this deficit, some of them radical, but none of them impractical.

First, and most simply, the discourse of diplomacy needs to be returned to earth. The pretentious and confusing terminologies of diplomacy must be simplified, and if possible, abandoned. When talking of globalisation, it might be simpler to talk about the homogenisation of global cultures, the liberalisation of capital markets, the movement of labour, or whatever it is we mean by the term rather than one that is bandied about without specification. Instead of referring to WMD, we should talk about nuclear, biological or chemical weapons and their vastly different qualities and capabilities, rather than a word designed to confound and terrify.[2] The UN Security Council should refer to "private meetings" rather than "informal consultations of Council members". And its public meetings should genuinely be public. The public is allowed to attend the legislatures of many democracies around the world; they should be allowed here too. Bureaucrats in places like the European Union must strive at all times to simplify the ludicrously arcane language of multilat-

eral foreign policy machinery (CFSP is the EU's common foreign and security policy, or GASP, its acronym in German; COREPER, the committee of permanent representatives where much of the real intra-EU bargaining is done).

Second, the world of diplomacy badly needs ventilation, or it may risk extinction (see below). A new non-government organisation called Security Council Report[3] now publishes on the web detailed briefings and reports on past and future meetings of the UN Security Council. Its product is outstanding and very helpful to the many who are trying to understand the workings of that secretive organ. But it need not have taken an NGO to do this. The Council itself, and its large and generously-staffed Secretariat, could easily have agreed to provide such a service, which would help reinforce the legitimacy and effectiveness of the Council. The European Union and other major multilateral organs (the World Trade Organisation, the African Union) should do the same if they too are not to be seen as closed, unrepresentative and thus illegitimate.

Most simply of all, these institutions should publish lists of which official does what. It is still absurdly difficult to telephone the UN or EU or WTO and speak to anyone with responsibility for any particular issue, from Palestine to banana imports. At the national level, foreign ministries should do likewise. In the British Foreign Office, the office directory is a classified document. This has the effect of preventing the ordinary public from contacting those who are making policy decisions in their name.

The veil of privilege and secrecy that surrounds international diplomacy should be lifted. There is nothing special about diplomacy. It requires no particular genius to practice. The doors of diplomacy are closed in part to obscure this truth. The deference shown to dip-

lomats is no more necessary than the deference shown to ordinary government servants. The arcane nomenclatures of "Your Excellency", "Minister Counsellor" and other ornate titles, the diplomatic uniform, cockaded hats and ribbons worn by ambassadors at formal occasions, can be put into the museum displays where they belong with the other artefacts of previous centuries.

Third, more deliberate means of accountability need to be established. Diplomats should be open to scrutiny and held responsible for their decisions as anyone else. In Britain, the introduction of a Freedom of Information Act sent shudders around the diplomatic service. But in Britain, a very large amount of information is still concealed unnecessarily in the name of national security. Parliament debates foreign affairs in Foreign Office questions (known, obscurely, as "TOPS") only once a month. It is a ludicrous spectacle, where the Foreign Secretary works through a long list of pre-submitted questions from MPs at a breakneck pace, covering issues of enormous subtlety and complexity (from Palestine to Zimbabwe) with the briefest possible answers. Even then, he or she doesn't manage to answer all the questions. But at least the Foreign Secretary appears in Parliament, the US Secretary of State doesn't do questions in the full Senate or House of Representatives.

At least in the US, ambassadors are quizzed by congressional committees before appointment (in Britain, there is no such system). But even here, the Senate and House are kept out of the inner business of the State Department and other agencies of international affairs. Somehow, everyone has grown to accept that it is not the public's business.

In both America and Britain, the legislatures appoint committees to scrutinise foreign policy. In both countries, reflecting the

snobbery and élitism of diplomacy itself, appointment to such a committee is reserved for the most senior and experienced senators and members of parliament (who tend immediately to mimic the pompous intonations of ambassadors and other "statesmen" in their commentaries). In the US, these committees are well-staffed and funded; in the UK, the Foreign Affairs Committee is so under-resourced that it can only manage to examine a few issues every year (it therefore tends to choose issues of meaningless generality like the "war on terrorism" or "globalisation"), although its funds, happily for its members, do stretch to vital "information-gathering" visits (where the diplomats organising them are careful to book expensive hotels and leave plenty of time for "shopping" in the programmes). But in both countries their work is limited to the separated territory known as international relations.

If we acknowledge the reality that almost every policy is in some way about what's going on in the rest of the world, the international element should be integrated both into government and its checks and balances, across the board. Instead, at the moment, it is separated and treated as a special discourse unto itself with its own special rules, words and traditions. Indeed, this élitism is a function of this separation. In order to validate an unjustifiable separation (and immunity from scrutiny), diplomats must constantly affirm their élite status.

Here's the most radical suggestion. We should consider abolishing the separate cadre of diplomats altogether. When international communication and arbitration is ever more necessary, we should divest ourselves of diplomats.[4] There are ten good reasons why:

1. The existence of diplomats reaffirms the separated nature of diplomacy and international relations from other areas of policy, when in fact they are inextricably connected.

2. Diplomats tend to be generalists and unskilled in the complexities of the global issues, from trade to terrorism, which now dominate our world. (The meagre two weeks I spent on induction training before starting work is very revealing in this respect.) Although I spent four and a half years reading intelligence on Iraq's weapons and arguing about them with other diplomats, my knowledge was inferior to life-long experts.[5] On issues such as global warming, both the science and the policy are beyond the grasp of diplomats who may only be appointed for temporary periods to handle negotiation. On terrorism, I well remember my embarrassment listening to my then ambassador attempting at the UN General Assembly to overcome decades-long argument over the definition of terrorism by offering this designation: "If it looks like a terrorist, if it acts like a terrorist, if it *smells* like a terrorist, then it is a terrorist" (emphasis was his).

3. It is ridiculous to pretend that the wishes and needs of an entire country can be embodied in a single diplomat, or embassy, or ambassador. The idea that an individual can accurately prioritise or balance these requirements, especially in the absence of any scrutiny, is unjustified. This was conceivable in the eighteenth century when the international needs of a country were much simpler and fewer (and where, absent democracy, the populations had little choice but to accept it); it is inappropriate for the vastly-connected era we now live in.

4. We need instead to promote multiple links at multiple levels between governments, avoiding the narrowing and outdated struc-

tures of traditional diplomacy. In some ways this is already happening. (I was struck for instance during my posting in Germany in the early 1990s that the Chancellor refused to see ambassadors — he considered them irrelevant.) In Europe, domestic ministers do a great deal of business directly with one another through the European Union, avoiding the traditional embassies altogether (albeit through the creation of a whole new set of impenetrable multilateral machineries). Ministries of environment now increasingly handle discussion of environmental issues, including global warming or ozone depletion. As international aspects intrude onto domestic policy, domestic ministries are taking over the traditional preserves of the diplomats. This process could usefully be accelerated.

5. Likewise, diplomats on the ground have not proved very skilful at monitoring local political trends. The British embassy in Tehran failed to notice the emerging revolution in Iran in 1979. Despite the lessons from that episode (to his credit, the then British ambassador taught others how to avoid his mistakes[6]), the embassy again failed to predict the electoral victory of President Mahmoud Ahmadinejad in 2005. Why this happens is easy to see, and has little to do with the personal skill of those individuals concerned. Diplomats tend to be posted for short periods; usually only a minority are trained in local languages. Their need for comfort and, increasingly, security tends to place them in secure, expat enclaves where they have little contact with the "locals". This is of course especially true in those countries least like our own (Pakistan, China) and where, arguably, we have the greatest need to understand (postings to such "difficult" posts tend to be shorter too). This task is therefore perhaps better performed by real country experts, fluent in local languages and

steeped in local custom, than the temporarily-posted diplomat. Already, an NGO called the International Crisis Group[7] (ICG) is deploying such analysts in the trouble spots of the world. The ICG has also taken the radical step of employing local experts (ex-journalists, political scientists and the like) to interpret what's going on. Thus, the ICG's reports are often more sophisticated and better informed than the "internal political" telegrams I produced and read as a diplomat (even though the latter are often classified, and the former are available on the worldwide web). After the riots which shook Kosovo in 2004, I accompanied the UN Special Representative around the UN headquarters in New York to explain what had gone wrong. All of those whom we spoke to, including senior members of the Department of Peacekeeping Operations (DPKO) referred to the ICG report (produced by a Briton with years of regional experience and a local Kosovar) rather than the UN's own reporting from the field. It was more objective (and critical of the UN) and simply better.

6. Diplomats have an existential interest in preserving the secretive traditions of diplomacy, which exclude outsiders, in order to maintain the mystique and status of their rôle. The more threatened by outside intrusion they become, the tighter they will close their doors. This tendency is already evident in the UN Security Council, where those who are resisting calls for more public meetings complain that publicity will drive the "real diplomacy" (i.e. the sort of cantankerous discussion described in chapters 3 and 8) out of these forums and into more private places. This argument is true but it is insufficient. What states want to keep secret they will, and they always have done.

7. The existence of diplomats tends to reaffirm the state-centric "realist" way of thinking about international relations. The diplomat is the international exponent of his state (not his government). This way of thinking accentuates and emphasises difference by forcing the practitioners to define their positions in terms of nation-states and anachronistic and invented identities (see chapter 5 "Them and Us"). It also rests on and continually reinforces Hobbesian notions of how the world works, i.e. of perpetual chaos without the enforcing hand of the state. These ways of thinking are circular (the state provides security; there is no security without the state) and can exacerbate, not reduce, conflict (the concept of pre-emptive war stands as the pre-eminent example). To take one example, in the debate in the UN Security Council on sanctions on Iraq, difference between the diplomats was habitual (and bitter) to the extent that we could barely imagine agreeing. In 2001, we had to agree a "control list" of items to be prohibited for export to Iraq. Such was the technical complexity of the items concerned, the diplomats had to leave the negotiation to experts in dual-use goods and other military technology. To the diplomats' great surprise, these experts were able quite easily to agree the list, over which the diplomats hitherto had argued for months. To them, it was relatively straightforward to agree what was potentially risky to export to Saddam's Iraq and what not.

8. This state-centric "realist" way of thinking is inherently amoral, and forces its exponents, including diplomats like me, to abandon their own personal moral sense. In long-serving diplomats, the morality of the state tends to subsume entirely any personal moral sensibility (or submerge it to the point of invisibility). It is continually

reinforced in the organs of diplomacy, such as the British Foreign Office, that the morality of the state, which is a form of immorality, is seen as superior to personal morality (*raison d'état* etc. etc.). This creates the possibility of bad, immoral policy such as sanctions on Iraq, or the Security Council's treatment of the Western Sahara, which make perfect sense in the "realist" security-centred way of thinking, but very little moral sense in terms of minimising human suffering or resolving disputes. Ordinary government servants, who lack the elevated status of diplomats, and who tend to be closer to the concerns of ordinary people, one hopes, are better immunised against this amoral sensibility.

9. While we are not about to get rid of the state, we should recognise the importance of, and give more weight to, the many other actors involved in international affairs. The existence of diplomats at the top of the pile tends to squeeze out these other actors, to the detriment of inclusive and thus effective policy-making. Governments like to think that they are in charge of world events. Diplomats exist, and have a strong self-interest, in reaffirming this solipsistic world view. Their dispatches and telegrams (even today, as you will see when they are eventually released) are full of grandiose statements about how this or that world problem might be solved (the omnipotent "we" again). This flatters the egos of the politicians whom they serve; it flatters their own egos. But they are wrong. Governments and diplomats are as much (if not more) impotent witnesses to world events as they are instigators. History suggests that even the ultimate preserve of government — war-making — has myriad and unpredictable antecedents and consequences. Governments are far from wholly in charge. The organisation of

government internationally and of international affairs generally should better reflect this reality.

We will still need embassies to organise ministers' visits and look after distressed travellers who lose their passports (indeed, as tourism swells, we will doubtless need more). There's no reason why embassies cannot still try to provide good on-the-ground analysis of what's going on, despite their inevitable limitations (indeed, this need is all the greater as decision-making is concentrated in capitals and the remove from reality increases). But already in the European Union (EU), the embassies of other EU members are becoming like bus terminals for visiting delegations of home government servants and ministers as they visit their opposite numbers in ever-increasing numbers. Groups of businesspeople come and go, using the embassy as they would an exclusive club, to impress their customers and business contacts (government-favoured businesses, notably the arms industry, tend mostly to benefit from this privilege). The ambassadors in such embassies, who have to put up with streams of official visitors using their residences for accommodation, have become glorified hotel managers, laying out the fancy crockery with tedious frequency.[8] The days of the professional diplomat as it once was conceptualised, the grand plenipotentiary representing *in toto* the political needs of his country in another state, are numbered if not already past.

10. Meanwhile, for the ordinary public, the self-serving élitism and fake-omnipotence of the world's diplomats has created a comforting illusion: that they are in control, allowing the rest of us to get on with our lives. We are not entitled to this illusion. The pact of irresponsibility must end. We must correspondingly take more

responsibility for our own international affairs. Our votes, and our behaviour, have international consequences. Every action, whether buying fruit, employing a cleaner, or choosing where to take your holiday is international, and is, in its way, a form of diplomacy. Everyone is a diplomat.

For obvious reasons, commercial companies have been the first to adapt to this reality. Bosses of big banks and manufacturers now visit China far more often than do our politicians (and thus know much more about it). Multinationals have long ago transcended the bounds of national location and identity. Exxon Mobil has a large political department to monitor and negotiate with the many governments with whom the company has dealings. McDonalds and Google are effectively conducting their own diplomacy, such are the multiple effects (local, international, social, economic, aesthetic, environmental) of their decisions. It was notable that during his 2006 visit to the US, Chinese President Hu Jintao visited Microsoft in Seattle before — and for longer than — he visited the Capitol. Watching the visit, I was struck by how Bill Gates squired the President around in the same manner an ambassador would have of old. Shareholders and consumers should be aware of this in their choices.

Some commentators on this trend, notably Thomas Friedman, argue that this massive commercial interaction is bound to have positive effects, that the internet for instance can only promote openness and free speech. Reality suggests that commerce and technology can be as ambiguous in their effects as anything else. Google, Yahoo and Microsoft have all been accused by Amnesty International[9] of abetting censorship and repression in China by supplying equipment and adapting their search engines to block certain sites and, in Yahoo's case, assisting the Chinese authorities in identify-

ing on-line anti-government critics. In response, they have argued that no company alone can change Chinese law, by which they must abide. The solution is therefore obvious.[10]

These forces must be pointed in the right direction if they are to be for the good. Effective foreign policy, whether in promoting labour rights or environmental standards, now requires coalitions of actors — the private sector, civil society and government — acting in concert to be effective.[11] If foreign ministries are to be effective, even relevant, in the future, as propagators of policy and change they must consider how to organise such coalitions, and how to encompass, direct and inform these many different strands and effectors of policy.

The NGO Global Witness has been tracking how wars are fuelled by the exploitation of natural resources — timber, diamonds — by unscrupulous governments and traders. Global Witness popularised the notion of "conflict diamonds", whose extraction (often in conditions of dreadful cruelty) was controlled by warlords in West Africa (Liberia's Charles Taylor being the most infamous example) but bought by international diamond trading companies and sold on the high street. The proceeds went to buy AK-47s and rocket-propelled grenades which were then used in the vicious and destructive wars in Liberia, Sierra Leone and elsewhere. Global Witness's work has done much to highlight a connection that both stimulates and sustains conflict, and as a result, governments and, to a limited extent, the diamond trade itself are having to take action. There is a long way still to go towards global rules and norms to inhibit such trade. The fact that Global Witness is run on a shoestring (its founders raised their first funds by shaking collecting tins at underground sta-

tions) and funded by philanthropic foundations illustrates that its ideas are still outside the foreign policy mainstream.

The practice and process of diplomacy, then, needs to change into something much more diverse and eclectic, such that we perhaps shouldn't give it a collective name — such as *diplomacy* — at all.

Beyond this transformation of diplomacy, there are other steps too, which involve a conscious abandonment of the state-centred thinking so intrinsic to the nature of international relations and diplomacy today. This touches on the substance, more than the process, of international relations. Here we must step into more idealist territory.

Cosmopolitanism dates from Greek society in the fourth century BC. A cosmopolitan is a citizen of the world — someone whose loyalties transcend a particular state or polity. As argued in more recent expositions,[12] cosmopolitanism embodies the idea that we have obligations to other human beings outside our nation, and that we must take seriously the ways in which people in different cultures choose to live. We may not agree with them, but we have to deal with them.

In a world of massive interaction, it seems we have little choice. In our world today, how the Russian government treats the Chechens may affect our safety riding the subway in London or New York City. Working conditions in Pakistan affect employment in Europe. Carbon emissions in Australia may endanger biodiversity in Sussex or Utah, or cause sea levels to rise in Bangladesh. Less selfishly, our emotions are touched by the suffering in Darfur.

Meanwhile, many of the things that most worry us, and undermine both our sense of well-being and our actual safety, do not fit into the conventional measurement of classical economics or theories of international relations. Our concern for the suffering of others, for

instance, is not easily quantified,[15] and nor is our instinct for nature — a profound human characteristic that has no measure in economic theory but has been demonstrated in countless studies. There are things beyond measure, beyond calculation. No one calculating Britain's or America's interest in not intervening in Bosnia in the early 1990s would have considered their decision's effect on the antipathy of Muslims in Egypt (or Leeds), sometimes many years later.

In the morass and confusion of forces at work in the twenty-first century, we need guideposts to steer our path. The intuitions and prejudices of less-connected eras are a help, but insufficient. As Tony Blair has said, we are looking at a world as an ever-changing kaleidoscope. As we are dazzled by its many colours and shapes, we still need criteria by which to make decisions — to guide us.

In contrast to the eclecticism I advocate for the future of diplomacy, we badly need singular if not to say universalist ideas of how to treat one another and arbitrate our global existence: common norms, if not common rules. Such universalism is naturally perilous. Many of our shared problems are classic "tragedies of the commons" where corrective action implies costs for the actor (such as a carbon tax), and where "free riding" is rewarded. Invoking singular standards immediately draws an accusation of the very essentialism I have earlier attacked.

Since Russia's government bears no cost directly (in electoral terms) for brutality in Chechnya (even if New York City may), what motive does it have to change policy? Put simply, the problem bedevilling international policy is that those deciding it are very often not those affected by it.

Here, Popper might guide us once more. The realist, interests-based model of national foreign policy-making encourages competi-

tive, short-term and ultimately counter-productive policy. Moreover, as Popper demonstrated, it is futile for any government, even on the well-trodden ground of domestic policy, to claim it knows what is right to do: knowledge is inevitably imperfect, so there must inevitably be error in policy-making. Instead, he proposed a simple criterion as the starting point for policy-making: the minimisation of suffering. This is an inversion of the normal calculus of policymaking: what do we want? Popper argued it is impossible to know the sum of human wants, they are so varied and sometimes unknowable. Policymaking should therefore start at the other end.

This criterion does not give us specific guidance in each case — how should we minimise suffering in Darfur? — but it orients us on the aim and the starting-point of policy, rather than flailing around in a welter of differing objectives ("security", "stability" "freedom" — to which the query is always raised, whose?). The details of any policy can only be worked out in the closest possible encounter with the facts, the reality, of any situation, avoiding as much as possible imposed intellectual models and metaphors, beyond this broad objective. It is also a universal objective, un-possessed by any one culture or religion, and therefore one on which the world community can, perhaps, agree. This is not to dispose of the law and mechanisms of human rights, development and the other motors for the betterment of humanity, but to try to regroup them in a new collective heading, to which all can agree. Our present discord needs a new consensus.

Even if such a common aim could be agreed, we would still need some kind of organisation to deliver it. Sadly, our institutions for international cooperation, above all the UN, are in bad shape. The scandal of the oil-for-food programme has undermined public con-

fidence in the UN, already weakened by the routine criticism of the Right in the US, which is so sceptical of international law and collective action. My own experience working in a UN field mission confirmed that it remains an institution internally riven by favouritism and inefficiency[14] (I remember one senior member of the mission advising me that, if I wanted a career in the UN, to spend my time cultivating senior "friends" in the UN system rather than doing my job). Meanwhile, for many other countries outside the closed circle of the P5, the UN's authority is weakened by the unrepresentativeness of the membership of its most powerful organ, the Security Council, and, as a result, the arbitrariness and injustice of many of its decisions (or lack of decisions). Its legal and moral authority is thus much the less.

Any reform must therefore tackle these twin problems. The non-western world tends to suspect "management reform" as camouflage for US attempts to weaken the UN (a suspicion fed by the appointment of a US ambassador to the UN who is famously hostile to it) when such reform is urgently necessary. The UN leadership (the Secretary-General and others) claim that much as they wish to reform, they cannot without the membership's consent (when in fact there is much that they could do internally without seeking political agreement). Reform needs to be packaged, in a new compact (maybe a new San Francisco conference, like the one where the UN was founded), with expansion of the Council membership and constitutional reform of the charter. This might address the sensible conclusions of the Secretary-General's High-Level Panel, whose recommendations, *inter alia* to update international law on the use of force, languish unimplemented.

Security Council reform is famously difficult, and has failed at several attempts, mainly because the candidates for membership cannot agree who should join (and for every candidate there is an equally hostile "anti-candidate" who wishes to see them fail, namely India (opposed by Pakistan), Germany (Italy), Japan (China) etc.) and because of the lack of enthusiasm from the P5, who, while often mouthing support for expansion, quietly prefer the privileges of the status quo (their veto power). They must realise that the erosion of the authority of the UN is already the result of this complacency.

As the UN's Deputy Secretary-General Mark Malloch Brown has argued,[15] the US recognises, but all too rarely acknowledges publicly, that it is a major beneficiary of the UN in all kinds of ways (cut-price peacekeeping for one, in places where the US does not wish to send its own troops). More broadly, all democracies have an interest in maintaining the international rule of law: without it, we're in the jungle. Do we want a world where communist (if that's the right word) China feels untrammelled by global rules, any more than it does already?

But, as I have argued, the crisis of diplomatic legitimacy has deeper roots than the complaints of mere governments. Our problems are global and we need a global politics to deal with them. The UN is an organisation of governments, and as it is currently constituted, it can never become a democratic organ. Even if every member state were democratic, it would still entail the problem of all inter-governmental bodies, namely that it operates at several removes from the reality of those whose lives it arbitrates. Those negotiating its policy would inevitably be required to pay more heed to the needs of other governments than the people affected by the policy. They must, if they are to reach decisions on anything.

Some global conferences — on the environment, and trade — have opened forums for NGOs to participate, albeit with no decision-making power. But NGOs have their own crisis of legitimacy too — whom do they represent? Mass membership organisations (Greenpeace, Amnesty International) have an answer to this challenge, but others do not or they represent positions which are not discussed with their memberships: they are far from democratic. In any case, no government will ever be willing to give NGOs, however democratic, equal influence on policy-making.

Often these NGOs have evolved and express themselves as single-issue campaigns — to ban landmines, or to end poverty. No one can deny the importance of these causes. But they cannot admit the complexity and interlinkage of contemporary problems. The Live 8 campaign was a compelling example of a widely-shared concern expressed as an all-too-simple solution. The multiple dimensions of any serious policy challenge, from ending poverty to tackling terrorism, lend themselves poorly to a narrowly-based campaign. Sending a text message "to the G8" does not amount to real political engagement.

We also must confront Isaiah Berlin's assumption, which is all the more true in a diverse and complex world, that no priority can always be absolute. Politics is a business of trade-offs and compromise, where human needs and desires must sometimes yield to one another. This is the essence of good politics — the discussion, the choosing, the decisions — tested against democratic scrutiny. In short, we need a global politics.

Global movements address single issues. Only global political parties can begin to deal with the complex. Only parties, elected in some way, can claim the fullest legitimacy to speak for people, a problem NGOs will always be challenged by. Global political

parties may seem hopelessly utopian, but the idea is unavoidably logical. Only parties can legitimately claim to represent those who choose them, or pay their membership dues. Only a global politics can lift us above the zero-sum games of governments short-sightedly arbitrating their "interests" in international forums.

This is not to advocate the immediate establishment of a world parliament. Institutions cannot simply be invented to solve a problem. They have to evolve, and become accepted as legitimate. The European Parliament has suffered from this very problem since its inception: founded as the élite's answer to the problem of the "democratic deficit" of the European Community (as it was then known), it has struggled for popular acceptance, not helped by the gross extravagance of its procedures and members. Institutions should be wanted, not designed.

A start might be made with the evolution of campaigns into parties. And as they evolve, a chamber might be established to sit alongside the General Assembly of the UN:[16] not (yet) a parliament, but an elected body of individuals, which would offer advisory resolutions on topics under discussion at the Council and GA. It would not have power to decide (this would be too much to ask): as the European Parliament has shown, you do not create legitimate or popular institutions by simply giving them powers; rather, they must develop and become accepted as legitimate first. Elections to this body must be democratic — thus encouraging democracy around the world — and proportional to population in order to avoid the imbalance of the General Assembly, where small countries outnumber the votes of the large, though they are together much smaller in population.

To avoid the grotesque costs (and resulting unpopularity) of the European Parliament, the new body might meet mostly on-line, by video-conference, with only occasional formal meetings in rotating cities, thereby also avoiding the creation of a new cadre of parasitical expatriates located in some expensive international capital. This chamber might have a limited life, ten years perhaps, to see whether it can become a respected and influential forum for international discussion. If it passes the test, a further international conference might grant it initial and limited powers (perhaps starting with co-decision on the UN budget), which might accrete as time goes on (it should be a long process). A massive leap of the imagination, for sure, but a dose of idealism is perhaps what we need right now.

This book has criticised the unwarranted and unscrutinised power of unelected officials who deal — often badly — with ever more of our collective business. The only long-term answer is for elected representatives to take their place. It is odd that this idea should seem today so far-fetched, when our shared problems so urgently demand wise collective decisions by actors we regard and accept as legitimate. The alternative is more bad decision-making, institutions that will continually struggle for authority and effect, and, in parallel, many people whose problems are not addressed, who feel disenfranchised, and thus disposed to violence to air their grievances. Framed this way, the direction we should travel is obvious.

As I end this book, I find myself again offering grandiose solutions to other people's problems, much as I did as a diplomat. Perhaps I should say simply this. I found that traditional diplomacy — the way the world's business is done — as I practised it in the British foreign service, left me, in the old sense of the word, "demoralised" — bereft of my own principles and sense of meaning. The system

I helped to manage and defend seemed to me out of kilter with the world's reality, and what was most important to me. In working for other countries and peoples, and getting to know their needs first rather than imposing "our" chosen solutions (invariably without consulting them), I have found more meaning and value than the exposition of "our" desires, which were in practice often invented, ever did. I can't offer it as an example for everyone: I wouldn't assume to know what they are like. But it worked for me.

NOTES

1. Introduction

[1]   Belgium, the Netherlands and Luxembourg.

[2]   A much-misused term, but in this context it meant chemical, nuclear and biological weapons, and missiles of over 150km range.

[3]   The United Nations Monitoring, Verification and Inspection Commission: this is my footnote in history since I invented UNMOVIC's name, late one night during the negotiations on Security Council resolution 1284 (1999), which established the agency.

[4]   We must all be grateful to President George W. Bush who, albeit inadvertently, revealed the truth of the direct and demotic nature of real diplomacy at a G8 summit in July 2006. Overhead on a microphone, he tells Prime Minister Tony Blair (after thanking him for the gift of a sweater) that the solution to the Lebanon crisis was "to get Syria to get Hizbollah to stop doing this shit". The President is far from alone in using such language. It is a common misperception that the behaviour and speech used in diplomacy are refined, elegant and measured (indeed the adjective "diplomatic" is used to describe such language). In reality diplomacy is often much more crude and harsh. For example, I was once told by a senior Asian ambassador: "I would rather be fucked up the arse with a rusty spoon than agree with you, Carne".

227

2. The Embassy

1 Samantha Power's *A Problem from Hell: America and the Age of Geno-cide*, London: Flamingo, 2003, is particularly good.

2 It didn't help that of course we only had a full embassy in Belgrade, the capital of what was once Yugoslavia. Inevitably the reporting from there tended to reflect the Belgrade view of affairs. There were no posts in Zagreb, Sarajevo or Pristina. This is another way in which the "statist" view of the world contributed to our misunderstanding of that debacle.

3 This was that in German law, thanks to Germany's history of shifting borders (only "finalised" with reunification in 1990), citizenship is conferred by parentage (or race) not place of birth (*ius sanguinis* as opposed to *ius soli*), and thus ethnicity and religion become especially important in determining German-ness. This explains why a child born to Turkish parents, even if raised in Germany with German as its "natural" language, is not considered German, legally by the state or culturally by many if not most Germans. Another consequence was that a Russian of originally German stock (even if many generations previously) had an immediate right to German citizenship, while a Turk born in Germany, even if second or sometimes third generation, did not. One shocking piece of evidence supporting the theory is that German immigration officials were reportedly using lists of German settlers in Russia prepared by the SS in the Second World War to check the veracity of claims by Russians claiming German heritage.

4 At the request of the Foreign and Commonwealth Office, amendments have been made to this chapter to protect national security, as they have elsewhere in the book.

5 There are some, more expert on Afghanistan than me, who argue that a policy premised upon a strong centre and subordinate regions was naïve in the first place as it failed to acknowledge the

fragmented and essentially tribal nature of the country where all are minorities. A better strategy, they argue, would be to build a more decentralised structure. See, for an example, "The Myth of 'One Afghanistan'", Charles Santos, *Los Angeles Times*, May 25, 2003.

3. The Negotiation (1)

[1] In recent years at the UN in New York it has become fashionable to call the non-permanent Council members, who serve on the Council for a two-year temporary term, "elected" members to emphasise their supposed legitimacy in contrast to the unelected status of the Permanent Five (P5) countries (the US, France, Russia, China, the UK). I have chosen not to use the term "elected" since it is inaccurate when most of the ten temporary members are not elected in contested elections, but are given seats by rote according to their regional group and place in the alphabet. Only two of the five countries elected every year win their seats through competitive elections of the UN membership, which are themselves often stitched up through backroom deals between countries.

[2] You will not find in this chapter a discussion of the Oil-for-Food "scandal" that has erupted in recent years. On this I have nothing to add to the excellent Volcker report (to which I testified at length).

[3] This term, now familiar to many, comprises non-conventional weapons including chemical, biological and nuclear ones. In Iraq's case it also meant ballistic missiles over 150km range (the full details were set out in "the mother of all resolutions", Security Council resolution 687, which in 1991 set out the precise terms of Iraq's obligations).

4   I hesitate to confess that the delegates responsible for negotiating a
     particular issue in the Security Council are called "experts" in the
     unofficial yet traditional nomenclature of that organ. I hesitate to
     confess it because of course most of us, myself included, were not
     expert, having no first-hand knowledge whatsoever of the coun-
     tries we were dealing with.

5   She said this during a television interview on the BBC.

6   The term "Arab street" is one that remains common in western
     diplomatic descriptions of the Middle East, despite Edward Said's
     compelling attack on such Orientalist depictions. Like other such
     locutions, it reveals far more about its user than what it purports
     to describe. When reading it, one can safely assume that the origi-
     nator has been nowhere near the "street", wherever that may be.

7   See, for example, "Ssh, they're arguing", Barbara Crossette, *New
     York Times*, 17 June 2001.

8   The word prohibition is a simplification since the import of the
     goods by Iraq was not explicitly prohibited in any case except that
     of purely military items, but the export of those goods on the list
     was to be *reviewed* by the UN sanctions committee (a sub-commit-
     tee of the Security Council) and possibly approved if the Commit-
     tee judged the end-use of those goods to be legitimately civilian.

9   These are discussed in chapter 4 below, but in general amount to
     the more rigorous enforcement not of generalised trade sanctions
     but of specific, targeted measures against the Iraqi government's
     illegal export of oil (through Turkey, Syria and the Gulf) and the
     stricter enforcement of import controls at Iraq's borders. A further
     technique was the aggressive pursuit of the regime's illegal finan-
     cial holdings abroad. None of these measures was ever properly or
     energetically pursued by either the UK or US governments, thus
     helping to create the situation where sanctions not only failed to
     force Iraqi compliance but also produced negative humanitarian
     consequences, a doubly bad policy.

4. War Stories

[1] A version of this chapter first appeared in the *Financial Times*, 29 January 2005.

[2] This was the official British inquiry into the use of intelligence on Iraq's WMD headed by Lord Butler, to which I testified in the summer of 2004.

[3] The Volcker Inquiry into the oil-for-food scandal found no such evidence.

5. Them and Us

[1] Game metaphors have been common in theories of international relations for some time. "Domino Theory", for example, proposed, erroneously as it turned out, the idea that if one country fell to communism, its neighbours would "tip over" into communism in an unstoppable chain reaction. Domino Theory was one of the main justifications for US involvement in Vietnam.

[2] This policy was thankfully soon changed, largely as a result of pressure from the unions. Britain now has its first openly gay Ambassador (though there were presumably many gay Ambassadors — albeit in the closet — before).

[3] As George Lakoff has asked in *Whose Freedom?*, New York: Farrar, Straus and Giroux, 2006.

[4] Since this debacle, it has been commonplace for British officials to claim that the threatened French veto blocked the resolution. In fact, there is no evidence that the draft resolution had attracted close to the nine votes required to pass in any case. My own research with other countries on the Security Council at the time suggests the UK's true vote count was closer to six. In other words, the putative veto was irrelevant, as the resolution could not have been voted through in any case.

5   Most notably Brendan Simms's *Unfinest Hour: Britain and the Destruction of Bosnia*, London: Allen Lane 2001.

6   One extreme example of this delineation and separation of sides is described in chapter 3, "The Negotiation" (1).

7   The study was published in *Science*, 7 October, 2005.

8   See *The Economist*, 29 July 2006

9   See Philip E. Tetlock, *Expert Political Judgment: How Good Is It? How Can We Know?*, Princeton University Press, 2005.

6. The Telegram or How to Be Ignored

1   Wherever it is in the world, the British government, like the US government, operates on "Zulu time" otherwise known as GMT. This is one of the myriad small ways that a common identity is fused with that other great exponent of the state: the military, which operates on the same time system.

2.   This example, like that of Northern Ireland, is — I fear — another reason to believe that terrorism "works", at least in highlighting a particular dispute if not in resolving it.

3   Independent Diplomat (see chapter 9) now advises the Polisario Front on its diplomacy.

4   Layard, Professor Richard (Lord), "Happiness: Has Social Science a Clue?", Lionel Robbins Memorial Lectures, London School of Economics, March 2003.

5   *The Pew Research Center for the People and the Press 2002 Global Attitudes Survey*; *Gallup International Survey, the Voice of the People*, September 2002.

6   See chapter 4, "War Stories".

7   Quoted in the *Financial Times*, 28 May 2003.

8   See, for instance, Robert Cooper, *The Breaking of Nations*, London: Atlantic Books, 2004.

9   The British government now does consult "Muslim groups" but at
     no time during my work on the Islamic world did such consulta-
     tion take place.

10   Amnesty International Report on Morocco.

11   This cynicism is widely shared among diplomats. In my work
     on sanctions against Iraq in the so-called 661 Committee of the
     UN Security Council, one of the UK's fiercest and most skilled
     adversaries was a Russian diplomat named Alexsander S. He was
     beautifully fluent in English and articulate and meticulous in pick-
     ing apart our arguments. Upon getting to know him, I found that
     he evinced little or no faith in the system he was serving. For him,
     it was just a job, advocacy for the sake of advocacy, much as a
     lawyer. "It's all bullshit", he would say, making a wry face.

12   17 October 2006, Foreign Office Minister of State Kim How-
     ells gave the following answer to a parliamentary question: "The
     UK fully supports the efforts of the UN Secretary-General, Kofi
     Annan, and his Personal Envoy to Western Sahara, Peter Van
     Walsum, to assist the parties to achieve a just, lasting and mu-
     tually acceptable political solution, which will provide for the
     self-determination of the people pf Western Sahara. The UK is in
     regular contact with representatives of the parties to the dispute
     and the UN. The UK will continue to encourage all parties to
     engage with the UN process. There are, however, no plans for a
     UN referendum to be held in the near future."

7. The Ambassador

1   This portrait is an amalgam of ambassadors I have known.

2   The 1991 war was widely referred to in the West as the Gulf
     War, even though there had already been a long and much more
     bloody "Gulf War" between Iran and Iraq in 1980 -9.

3   See chapter 4, "Them and Us".

[4]   See John Gray's, *Straw Dogs: Thoughts on Humans and Other Animals*, London: Granta, 2004.

8. Star Trek, Wittgenstein and the Problem with Foreign Policy

[1]   Reproduced, with kind permission of the publisher, from Christopher Logue's, *War Music*, © Faber & Faber, 2001.

[2]   Ludwig Wittgenstein, *The Duty of Genius*, Harmondsworth: Penguin Books, 1991 reprinted edn.

[3]   George Lakoff's work on metaphor is instructive on all this.

[4]   In 2003, during a Middle East summit in Aqaba, President George W. Bush described how he deliberately steered Israeli Prime Minister Sharon and Palestinian Authority President Abbas out of the formal room in which they had been seated into the garden. "What I wanted to do is to observe the interplay between the two; did they have the capacity to relax in each other's presence for starters? And I felt they did." (Source: *Financial Times*, 6 June 2003.)

[5]   Nina Khruscheva of the New School has argued that culture never lies about politics even when politicians do, that for instance that while Donald Rumsfeld denies that the US has an imperial project, the contemporaneous movies *Troy*, *Alexander the Great* and *Kingdom of Heaven* tell a different story (*Financial Times*, 19 April 2006). I am not sure I would go as far as Khruscheva; *Capote*, *Brokeback Mountain* or *Crash* suggest rather different narratives.

9. The Negotiation (2)

[1]   Though I have lightly edited the piece, the style and content remain essentially the same as when I wrote it in January 2000.

[2] One night in New York, I had to come up with a new name for the agency, in part because agreement seemed to require that we change the name from that in the UK draft up till that point (this was the acronym, UNCIIM, for UN Commission for Inspection and Investigation and Monitoring, a word that, to Russian and French ears, sounded too much like one designed for the pursuit of criminals). We needed a new name that incorporated the key concepts of MOnitoring, Verification, Inspection and Commission. UNMOVIC was the construction which, after several hours of crossword-like pondering, I came up with.

[3] For the full text go to www.securitycouncilreport.org/atf/cf/%7B65BFCF9B-6D27-4E9C-8CD3-CF6E4FF96FF9%7D/

[4] Thomas S. Kuhn, *The Structure of Scientific Revolutions*, University of Chicago Press, 3rd edn, 1996.

[5] I would suggest that a classic example of this phenomenon, examined in chapter 2, is that of the break-up of Yugoslavia. It was not only the massacre of Srebrenica that produced a shift in the view of that war as a "civil war". It was psychologically impossible for the Conservative government, then in power, to admit this, but the massacre and the dawning understanding that the war was very much *not* a civil war produced a paradigm shift in the incoming Labour government which later adopted in Kosovo an altogether more interventionist approach.

10. Independent Diplomat or the Other Side of the Table

[1] Somalia, Kosovo and Western Sahara are all on the agenda of the UN Security Council.

11. Conclusion:
The End of "Diplomacy"?

1   GM is famously burdened by massive obligations — amounting
    to some $85bn — to fund the pensions of its former and current
    workers.

2   At the inquiry into the death of British weapons scientist (and my
    former colleague), David Kelly, one of the Ministry of Defence
    witnesses, Brian Jones, said "I think 'weapons of mass destruction'
    has become a convenient catch-all which in my opinion can at times
    confuse discussion of the subject."

3   www.SecurityCouncilReport.org

4   I am aware that this proposal will strike some as unrealistic. Trotsky
    gave us the notion of a "transitional idea", a demand that you know
    to be unrealisable in the current circumstance, but in making it
    you may nevertheless change the current system for the better, and
    ultimately it may be shifted to where the demand can be realised.

5   Who included, for instance, David Kelly on whom I and the UK
    Mission to the UN relied on heavily for expert interpretation of the
    evidence on Iraq's biological weapons programme. For instance, I
    asked him many times to brief other Security Council delegations
    on Iraq's weapons programmes, along with other British experts
    on chemical weapons and ballistic missiles. Somewhat belying the
    British government's portrayal of him after the infamous *Today* pro-
    gramme No. 10 dossier leak, we regarded him at the UK mission as
    Britain's foremost and most authoritative expert.

6   In brief, these were that the embassy had neglected on-the-ground
    political reporting in its rush to sell British goods to the Shah. Sir
    Anthony Parsons, the ambassador, argued that embassies should
    always ensure that they had diplomats fluent in local languages who
    were tasked to go out and listen to ordinary people. He also warned
    against the tendency in reports back to the capital to emphasise

developments favourable to our interests, and downplay less positive news.

7 www.crisisgroup.org

8 My ambassador in Germany once wearily told me that six nights
   out of seven he was either entertaining officially or attending official
   dinners.

9 *Amnesty International Report*, 20 July 2006

10 The Open Society Institute — not a government, note — is working with universities to develop a Code of Conduct for IT companies operating in China.

11 The UN's Global Compact was a start at this challenge, but it needs
   to be more widespread. The Global Compact was, by dint of who
   instigated it, not a mass activity.

12 Such as Kwame Anthony Appiah and Henry Louis Gates's *Cosmopolitanism: Ethics in a World of Strangers*, New York: W. W. Norton,
   2006.

13 An economist might argue that this concern is easily counted in the
   amounts individuals choose to give to charity, but this does not take
   into account reservations people may have — which may inhibit such
   giving — about the effectiveness of aid and other relevant factors.

14 Shirley Hazzard's, *People in Glass Houses*, London: Macmillan, 1967,
   reprinted 1996, shows that such problems are of depressingly long
   standing.

15 See his controversial speech "Power and Super-Power: Global
   Leadership in the Twenty-First Century", delivered at the Century
   Foundation and Center for American Progress — Security and
   Peace Initiative, New York, 6 June 2006.

16 Perhaps another "transitional idea".

INDEX

Adan, Edna 187-9, 197
Afghanistan 16, 36-46, 92, 104, 110-11, 200
African Union 194, 207
Ahmadinejad, Mahmoud 211
Al Qaeda 42-5, 71, 73, 200
Albania 95
ambassadors 129-32
Amnesty International 216, 223
Amorim, Celso 166
Australia 218
Austria 4
Aziz, Tariq 58

Baghdad 65, 133
Bagram 36, 44
Baker, James 113, 126
Bamiyan 40
Bangladesh 61
Basra 133
Berbera 187-8
Berger, Sandy 180
Berlin, Isaiah 123, 223
bin Laden, Osama 39, 53, 104
Blair, Tony 73, 76-7, 80, 219
Bonn 27-36, 111, 140

Bosnia 30-1, 93, 124, 219
Brazil 121, 166, 168, 177-8
Bush, President George W. 73, 76, 80, 144, 145, 148, 160
Butler, Richard 184
Butler inquiry 16, 73-4, 75, 76, 190

Callières, François de 102
Cambridge 87
Canada 97, 168, 177-8
Chechnya 104, 200, 218
Cheney, Dick 143
China 28-9, 61, 84, 95, 96, 99, 170, 176, 216-17, 222
Chirac, President Jacques 185
CIA 120
Clinton, President Bill 58, 183
Cold War 71, 89, 142
Cologne 33
Congo 162
Cook, Robin 75
Croatia 32
Czechs 97

Darfur 218, 220

"democratic deficit" 10-12, 20, 206, 224
diamonds 217
diplomacy: general comments 20-6, 101-3, 196, 203-26
Dostum, General 39, 41
drug smuggling 43-4

economic questions 116-19
Egypt 93, 94
Emergency Unit 132-7, 139
Ethiopia 188
European Parliament 224-5
European Union (EU) 4, 9, 10, 33, 93, 122, 145, 193, 194, 204, 206-7, 211, 215, 224
extraordinary rendition 126
Exxon Mobil 216

France 6-7, 51, 59-60, 61, 63, 64, 65, 93, 170, 173-4, 175-6, 182-5
Freedom of Information Act 208
Friedman, Thomas 216
Fukuyama, Francis 143

Gadhafi, Muammar 101
Gates, Bill 216
Germany 27-36, 62, 87, 96, 211, 222
Global Witness 217-18
globalisation 159, 160, 203-5, 206
Gombrowicz, Witold 8
Google 216
Greenpeace 223
Greenstock, Sir Jeremy 168
Group of Eight (G8) 121, 172, 223
Gulf War 1991 132-7, 139, 141, 168

Hamburg 34
Hargeisa 187-9
Hazaras 40-1
heroin 43-4
Hobbes, Thomas 142, 148, 213
Hu Jintao 216

IAEA 179, 183-4
immigrants and asylum seekers 28, 29-30, 34-5, 203-4
Independent Diplomat 25, 191-202
India 97, 222
intelligence 74-6
International Crisis Group 212
Iran 16, 45, 94, 101, 211
Iraq 13-17, 19, 50-70, 71-81, 132-41, 165-86, 210, 211, 213-14
Iraqi National Congress 75
Ismail Khan 39, 41
Israel 136, 139, 200
Italy 137, 205, 222

Jalalabad 110
Japan 222
Joseph Rowntree Charitable Trust 197

Kabul 38, 40, 41, 46
Kant, Immanuel 119, 138, 142-3
Karzai, Hamid 42
Kelly, David 14, 15-16
KGB 89
Khalili, Karim 40-1
Kissinger, Henry 142
Korea, North 148
Kosovo 2-6, 16, 19, 95, 97, 146-7, 172, 191-202

Kosumi, Bajram 2-6
Kuchi 44
Kuhn, Thomas 73
Kurds 51
Kuwait 55, 132-7, 166-7

language and discourse of diplomacy
     18, 21, 22, 23-4, 83-8, 156-62,
     206-7
Lavrov, Sergei 184
Layard, Richard 117
Leavitt, Theodore 159
liberal view of international relations
     142-3, 145-6
Liberia 217
Libya 101
Live 8 223
Locke, John 142
London bombs 200
Loya Jirga 39-43

MacDonald, Ramsay 75
Machiavelli, Niccolò 129, 141-2, 147-
     8
Malaysia 170, 176
Malloch Brown, Mark 222
Maslow, Abraham 117-18
McDonalds 216
Masood, Ahmed Shah 37
Microsoft 216
migration 28, 29-30, 34-5, 203-4
military operations in Afghanistan
     42-5
Mill, J.S. 142
Milosevic, Slobodan 6, 147
moral responsibility 138-40
Morocco 112-15, 125-8

Mubarak, President. 94
multinationals 216
Muslims 124, 219

NAM (Non Aligned Movement) 49
National Institute on Aging (NIA)
     97-8
National Security Council 120-1, 149
NATO 146-7
neo-conservatives 143-4
Netherlands 51, 168
New School University, New York 14
NGOs 55, 57, 207, 212, 217-18,
     222-3
Norway 2, 95-6, 155
Nye, Joseph 144-5

O'Neill, Tip 203
Official Secrets Act 90-1
oil 64, 77, 79, 168, 177, 183
Oil-for-Food programme 50-3, 166-
     7, 220-1
Open Society Institute 197
Operation Desert Fox 165, 172, 184
Operation Desert Storm 132-7
Oslo 155
Oxford Research Group 161

P5, *see* United Nations Security
     Council
Pakistan 37, 44, 218, 222
Palestinians 19, 139, 200
parliament (British) 127, 208, 209,
     212
Pilger, John 56, 66
Poland 89

Polisario Front 112-14, 193, 194, 197

Popper, Karl 10, 11, 70, 197, 201, 206, 219-20

Project for the New American Century 143

Putin, President. 185

Quayle, Dan 143

realist view of international relations 141-2, 145-6, 213-14

refugees 30, 114, 125

resignation (by author) 190

Rice, Condoleezza 84

Roma 34, 111

Rousseau, Jean-Jacques 142

Russia 51, 57-8, 60, 63, 64, 170, 172, 174-6, 182-5, 200, 218, 219

Rwanda 32-3

Saddam Hussein 14, 52, 69, 72, 73, 79, 80, 120

Said, Edward 95, 98

sanctions 13-14, 49-70, 76-9, 92, 167, 168, 172-5, 179-81, 183-6, 213-14

Saudi Arabia 104

Scud missiles 14, 73, 136

Seattle 216

Secret Intelligence Service (SIS) 73, 75-6

security questions 119-21

September 11 attacks 41, 73-4, 74, 79, 104, 148, 154, 199-200

Serbia, Serbs 3, 31-2, 144, 147, 192

Shah of Iran 45, 46

Shia Muslims 94, 135

Sierra Leone 204, 217

Silva, Luiz Inacio da 121

Singapore 93

Sinti 34

Slovenia 177-8

smuggling (Iraq) 77-9

Somaliland 97, 187-9, 194

Soros, George 197

South Africa 86

Soviet Union 37, 71, 89, 120

Spain 112

Srebrenica 32

Star Trek 155-6

Strauss, Leo 71, 80, 81

Tadic, Boris 3

Taliban 37, 39, 41, 42-5

Taylor, Charles 217

Tel Aviv 136

telegrams 81, 107-15, 126-7

Tetlock, Philip E. 103-4

Thatcher, Margaret 86

trade questions 116-19

trade talks 100-1

Tunisia 62

Turkey 93

UNICEF 52-3

United Nations 1-16, 39, 41, 49-70, 95, 112-15, 165-188, 190-2, 193, 194, 212, 220-2; General Assembly 171, 210, 224; Secretary-General 5, 9, 221; Security Council 1-7, 13-15, 17, 37, 49-70, 72, 77-8, 99-100, 112-13,

127, 147, 151-4, 162, 165-86, 190, 92, 206, 207, 221-2
UNMIK 3
UNMOVIC 15, 173, 179
UNPROFOR 31
UNSCOM 167, 170, 172-3
USA 4, 8-9, 31, 32, 39, 41, 44-5, 51, 55, 56, 57-63, 76, 78-9, 92, 97, 99, 104, 113-14, 120-1, 122, 128, 143-4, 148-9, 169-73, 175, 178, 180-5, 199-200, 208, 216, 219, 221-2

Versailles 6-7
vetting 88-90

"war on terror", *see also* Afghanistan 200

Weapons of Mass Destruction (WMD) 14-16, 51, 71-4, 76, 81, 133, 166-7, 170-6, 179-86, 190, 206
Weller, Paul 60-1
Western Sahara 112-16, 125-8, 193-5, 214
Wilson, Woodrow 144
Wittgenstein, Ludwig 19-20, 157-8, 160, 163
Wolfowitz, Paul 143
World Trade Organisation (WTO) 9, 100, 191, 207

Yahoo 216-17
Yugoslavia, former 6, 30-3, 126, 142, 144

Zinoviev Letter 74-5